Study Guide
to
Human Action
A Treatise on Economics

Study Guide

to

Human Action

A Treatise on Economics

Scholar's Edition

Ludwig von Mises

Robert P. Murphy
& Amadeus Gabriel

Auburn, Alabama

Copyright © 2008 by Ludwig von Mises Institute

All rights reserved. Written permission must be secured from the publisher to use or reproduce any part of this book, except for brief quotations in critical reviews or articles.

Published by the Ludwig von Mises Institute
518 West Magnolia Avenue, Auburn, Alabama 36832-4501
mises.org

ISBN: 978-1-933550-38-1

CONTENTS

PREFACE ix

PART ONE— HUMAN ACTION

CHAPTER 1— ACTING MAN 1

CHAPTER 2— THE EPISTEMOLOGICAL PROBLEMS OF THE
SCIENCES OF HUMAN ACTION 11

CHAPTER 3— ECONOMICS AND THE REVOLT AGAINST
REASON 23

CHAPTER 4— A FIRST ANALYSIS OF THE CATEGORY
OF ACTION 29

CHAPTER 5— TIME 37

CHAPTER 6— UNCERTAINTY 45

CHAPTER 7— ACTION WITHIN THE WORLD 53

*PART TWO— ACTION WITHIN THE FRAMEWORK
OF SOCIETY*

CHAPTER 8— HUMAN SOCIETY 63

CHAPTER 9— THE ROLE OF IDEAS .73

CHAPTER 10— EXCHANGE WITHIN SOCIETY 79

PART THREE—ECONOMIC CALCULATION

CHAPTER 11— VALUATION WITHOUT CALCULATION 85

CHAPTER 12— THE SPHERE OF ECONOMIC CALCULATION ..93

CHAPTER 13— MONETARY CALCULATION AS A TOOL
OF ACTION 101

*PART FOUR—CATALLACTICS OR ECONOMICS
OF THE MARKET SOCIETY*

CHAPTER 14— THE SCOPE AND METHOD OF
CATALLACTICS 105

CHAPTER 15— THE MARKET 115

CHAPTER 16— PRICES 133

CHAPTER 17— INDIRECT EXCHANGE 151

CHAPTER 18— ACTION IN THE PASSING OF TIME 175

CHAPTER 19— THE RATE OF INTEREST 193

CHAPTER 20— INTEREST, CREDIT EXPANSION, AND THE
TRADE CYCLE 205

CHAPTER 21— WORK AND WAGES 223

CHAPTER 22— THE NONHUMAN ORIGINAL FACTORS
OF PRODUCTION 239

CHAPTER 23— THE DATA OF THE MARKET 245

CHAPTER 24— HARMONY AND CONFLICT OF INTERESTS ..251

*PART FIVE: SOCIAL COOPERATION
WITHOUT A MARKET*

CHAPTER 25— THE IMAGINARY CONSTRUCTION OF
A SOCIALIST SOCIETY 257

Contents *vii*

CHAPTER 26— THE IMPOSSIBILITY OF ECONOMIC
CALCULATION UNDER SOCIALISM 263

PART SIX—THE HAMPERED MARKET ECONOMY

CHAPTER 27— THE GOVERNMENT AND THE MARKET 271

CHAPTER 28— INTERFERENCE BY TAXATION 279

CHAPTER 29— RESTRICTION OF PRODUCTION 283

CHAPTER 30— INTERFERENCE WITH THE STRUCTURE
OF PRICES 291

CHAPTER 31— CURRENCY AND CREDIT MANIPULATION . . .301

CHAPTER 32— CONFISCATION AND REDISTRIBUTION 313

CHAPTER 33— SYNDICALISM AND CORPORATIVISM 319

CHAPTER 34— THE ECONOMICS OF WAR 325

CHAPTER 35— THE WELFARE PRINCIPLE VERSUS THE
MARKET PRINCIPLE 333

CHAPTER 36— THE CRISIS OF INTERVENTIONISM 343

CHAPTER 37— THE NONDESCRIPT CHARACTER OF
ECONOMICS 347

CHAPTER 38— THE PLACE OF ECONOMICS IN LEARNING . .351

CHAPTER 39— ECONOMICS AND THE ESSENTIAL
PROBLEMS OF HUMAN EXISTENCE 359

INDEX 365

PREFACE

Murray Rothbard's massive *Man, Economy, and State with Power and Market* is the best single book for a fairly complete exposition of the modern Austro-libertarian worldview. Although Rothbard's prose is characteristically crystal clear, even so the book's daunting size intimidated many newcomers, leading to the regrettable situation where many self-identified Austrians hadn't read one of the most important books in the tradition. To address this grave condition, the Ludwig von Mises Institute commissioned me to write a study guide for *MES*.

The *MES* study guide was a success. It allowed new readers to test the waters before diving in, and at the same time it was a useful reference for experienced readers. I personally would use the guide whenever I prepared a lecture touching on some aspect of Rothbard's treatise.

The Mises Institute now hopes to do the same with the present study guide to Ludwig von Mises's *Human Action*. I will not here give a history or description of Mises's *magnum opus*, for those tasks are performed much more ably in the "Introduction to the Scholar's Edition" by Jeffrey M. Herbener, Hans-Hermann Hoppe, and Joseph T. Salerno. Suffice it to say, one cannot really claim to be an Austrian economist—certainly not a Misesian!—without reading *Human Action*. (And yes, you really need to read it cover to cover. It's all good.)

ix

The format of this study guide is straightforward. Each chapter starts with a summary that follows the numbered section headings and italicized subheadings as they appear in Mises's text. Then it provides an explanation of "Why It Matters," giving historical context and/or explaining the role that the chapter serves in the book. (One of the joys of writing this study guide was my discovery that there was a very systematic arrangement of the chapters and parts of the book, which I had not noticed during prior readings.) The next section provides "Technical Notes," which address difficulties in Mises's arguments, and clarifies subtle points. When relevant, this section also relates Mises's work to mainstream economics, for the benefit of graduate students or professors.

Finally, each chapter ends with a detailed list of "Study Questions," the bulk of which had been independently prepared by Amadeus Gabriel. I was very pleased to learn of Mr. Gabriel's efforts, because his questions ensure that the reader is grasping the essential points (some of which had to be ignored in the summary section), but also because his contribution allowed the completion of this study guide much sooner than would otherwise have been possible. (And as we all know, a present study guide is preferred to a future study guide.)

I hope the present guide encourages more people to read what is arguably one of the most important books written in the 20th century.

ROBERT P. MURPHY
Nashville, Tennessee
December 2008

Part One—Human Action

CHAPTER I

FUNDAMENTALS OF HUMAN ACTION

Chapter Summary

1. PURPOSEFUL ACTION AND ANIMAL REACTION

Human action is purposeful behavior. The distinguishing feature of action is that the observer imputes a *goal* to the actor. Action is different from purely reflexive behavior. A man may flinch after a loud noise. This is not necessarily action in the Misesian sense.

Praxeology is the science of action as such. That is, praxeology as a field contains all results that can be deduced from the fact that people have ends (i.e., goals), and adopt means of trying to achieve them. The specific *content* of the ends, and whether the means chosen are suitable, lie outside the scope of praxeology.

Every action is a *choice*, where the actor selects one alternative that he prefers to another.

2. THE PREREQUISITES OF HUMAN ACTION

In order for action to occur, the actor must be in a state of uneasiness or dissatisfaction. (If he were perfectly content, he would not act.) Along with the uneasiness, the actor must be able to imagine a more satisfactory state. Finally, the actor must believe that purposeful behavior has the power to remove or

1

reduce the uneasiness. If this last condition were lacking, the unhappy person would not act, since he would be unable to conceive of any way to improve his situation.

On Happiness

It is acceptable to view action as man's striving for "happiness." However, such a claim is liable to misinterpretation. In praxeology, *happiness* (or *utility*, or *satisfaction*) is a purely formal term, defined entirely by the subjective goals of the individual actor.

On Instincts and Impulses

Certain schools of thought reject praxeology as "rationalistic." Instead, these critics claim that people behave on instincts, just like other animals. There are two problems with this view. First, even if the critics were correct, and humans really did act on the basis of "instincts," nonetheless praxeology would still be valid. Acting on instinct is still action, and praxeology studies action as such, regardless of its underlying causes. A second problem with the instinct argument is that, unlike lower animals, humans clearly *can* suppress their biological urges. A martyr can choose to go to the stake rather than renounce his beliefs (thus violating the instinct of survival), and cash-strapped couples can use their reason to avoid the instinct to reproduce.

3. HUMAN ACTION AS AN ULTIMATE GIVEN

By its very nature, science will never be able to explain everything. Science proceeds by pushing back the limits of ignorance, but at any point a scientific discipline must start with assumptions or "givens," and then proceed (scientifically!) from there. In the scientific study of action, the ultimate starting point is action itself. Praxeology simply takes it for granted that action exists, and traces out the implications of this fact.

Chapter I: Acting Man   *3*

All studies of human actions must rely on *methodological dualism.* The second half of this phrase—"dualism"—simply means that there are apparently two different realms of causality. On the one hand is the physical material world, the structure and laws of which the physicists, chemists, and so on can describe with greater and greater accuracy. On the other hand, there is always the mental or subjective world, including thoughts, emotions, desires, and so forth. The first word in the phrase—"methodological"—signifies that Mises is not taking a stand on the ultimate philosophical dispute. That is, Mises concedes that the materialists might be correct; perhaps every thought really can be directly attributed to a configuration of atoms. Nonetheless, even if this is true in some cosmic sense, Mises argues that at present the "mind-body" connection is so poorly understood that praxeologists must adopt dualism if only for pragmatic reasons. It certainly seems *as if* people have free will and can truly *choose* among alternatives.

4. Rationality and Irrationality; Subjectivism and Objectivity of Praxeological Research

It is redundant to use the phrase "rational action," because all action is necessarily rational in that the actor uses means to (attempt to) achieve an end. By the same token, there is no such thing as an irrational action. Because praxeology takes preferences as given, it does not analyze their content. Some desires, such as those for food or shelter, are more common than others, yet this doesn't make the former more "rational." It is also wrong to condemn an action as irrational simply because the means chosen were ill suited to achieve the desired end. So long as the actor truly believes the means will achieve the end, the attempt to implement this causal relation is an action.

Praxeology exhibits *subjectivism* in that it takes actors' subjective ends as they exist in the minds of each person. By refraining from passing judgment on these ends, praxeology itself is objective.

5. CAUSALITY AS A REQUIREMENT OF ACTION

Causality is necessary for action, because without understanding cause and effect an actor could never hope to alter the flow of events and thus increase his happiness. The Heisenberg uncertainty principle and other developments in modern physics do not alter this.

6. THE ALTER EGO

All events must fall in the realm of teleology or causality. That is, all events must be ascribed either to the intentions of an actor or to the mechanical unfolding of physical law. Many thinkers are prejudiced against teleology, but, on their own terms, the positivists must admit that the assumption of the alter ego—that is, the assumption that there are other wills just as one is aware of his own will—is very pragmatic; it *works* better than to simply view the bodily movements of others as the complex outcome of chemical processes.

On the Serviceableness of Instincts

At first it would seem that an animal's instinctive behavior is a middle ground between teleology and causality. Yet "instinct" is simply a term to describe the motivation of which we are ignorant. Even the behaviorist unwittingly adopts the vocabulary of praxeology when analyzing animal behavior.

The Absolute End

Praxeology deals with the subjective ends of mortal men. It is irrelevant whether or not God or Manifest Destiny is moving human events toward some ultimate end.

Chapter I: Acting Man 5

Vegetative Man

Some philosophies, such as Buddhism, teach that happiness can be attained only when all goals are renounced. If a man were to truly achieve such a state of vegetative existence, he would cease to act and praxeology would no longer apply.

Why It Matters

Many times in *Human Action* the modern reader may be puzzled by the pains Mises takes in critiquing particular views that seem obviously fallacious, or by the lengths to which Mises defends particular views that seem obviously correct. The reader must understand that Mises is not inventing straw men or being paranoid; respected thinkers really *did* advance the views he attacks, and really *did* attack economics with weak criticisms.

Mises takes care in the very beginning (pp. 11–13) to distinguish rational action (a term he considers redundant, since action by definition is rational) from reflexive behavior. This is necessary because a very popular objection (pp. 15–16) to the enterprise of praxeology is the claim that people do not always behave "rationally," and that men often behave like other animals. To the extent that economics allegedly explains all human behavior as the product of sober deliberation, these critics think it is obviously unrealistic. By carefully limiting the scope of praxeology to human actions (rather than the more general class of all human behavior), *by definition* Mises has defused this particular criticism. (In subsequent chapters, Mises will have much more to say on the role of reason in human affairs.)

The passages concerning happiness (pp. 14–15) relate to the evolving doctrine of utilitarianism. In its original Benthamite form, the criterion for goodness was that which caused more (net) pleasure than (net) pain. Even here the utilitarians recognized that certain pleasures (such as fine art or literature) provided a longer duration of enjoyment than others (such as tobacco or wine). However, much of the literature did seem to be a sophisticated version of hedonism. Moreover, economists in the late 19th century tended to think of "utility" as a measurable quantity of psychic satisfaction. As Mises explains in this section, when he says that man acts to increase his happiness, this is a purely formal statement with no physiological assumptions. Both the bank robber and missionary act to increase their utility. What praxeology has to say about the actions of the former are just as valid for those of the latter, because praxeology concerns action as such.

Technical Notes

(1) Mises argues that an actor must believe "that purposeful behavior has the power to remove or at least to alleviate the felt uneasiness" (p. 14). This wording is ambiguous and might be too strong a requirement. In order to act, a person must merely believe that a particular choice will *possibly* alleviate the uneasiness. For example, a skeptical man with a terminal illness might, in desperation, consult a faith healer, even though he strongly doubts it will have any effect. (Although Mises's wording is actually consistent with such cases, other Austrian expositions explicitly—and erroneously—say that an actor must believe that his action will remove uneasiness. The present note is provided to remove any confusion.)

(2) There is some ambiguity in the discussion of ultimate givens. On the one hand, Mises clearly states that human action is an ultimate given; it is the title of section 3 (p. 17). On the other, praxeology has much to say on the necessary prerequisites for action; this is the title of section 2 (p. 13). One possible solution to this apparent contradiction is to recall that action is *not* simply the outward behavior of the actor; the action as such necessarily *includes* the subjective motivations of the actor as well. In this sense, it would be inappropriate to say that someone's value judgments "caused" an action; action is still an ultimate given and cannot be reduced to antecedent constituents. (For an

imperfect analogy: the homicide is not simply *caused* by the killer's hatred of the victim; without the intention it wouldn't be murder in the first place.)

(3) At times, Mises is not careful to distinguish limits on praxeology versus limits on reason itself. For example, Mises says that

> it is vain to pass judgment on other people's aims and volitions. No man is qualified to declare what would make another man happier or less discontented. (pp. 18–19)

Now it is true that praxeology as such does not analyze the content of people's values or preferences; it simply takes them as given. However, this alone doesn't mean "it is vain to pass judgment on other people's aims." Surely Mises himself disagreed passionately with, say, advocates of socialism, and one could infer that Mises did indeed condemn their aims. By the same token, parents all the time declare what would make their children happier, and surely these claims are not *always* incorrect (whatever the children might think at the time). To be on solid ground, one can say that no man can ever tell another man what his preferences are. Even so, there is nothing in praxeology that rules out a critique of another's preferences; it is simply that praxeology itself cannot fashion such a critique.

Chapter I: Acting Man

Study Questions

1. **Purposeful Action and Animal Reaction**

   - What distinguishes praxeology from psychology?
   - Why doesn't action consist merely in giving preference to something?
   - What does Mises mean by, "Action is a real thing"?

2. **The Prerequisites of Human Action**

   - What's always the incentive for a man to act?
   - What are the general conditions of human action?
   - Why is it a tautology to declare that a man's unique aim is to attain happiness?
   - What distinguishes man's behavior from animal behavior?

3. **Human Action as an Ultimate Given**

   Comment: "As [human action] cannot be traced back to its causes, it must be considered as an ultimate given and must be studied as such."

4. **Rationality and Irrationality; Subjectivism and Objectivity of Praxeological Research**

   - Why must the term "rational action" be rejected as pleonastic (i.e., redundant)?

- Why does the term "irrational" imply a value judgment?
- Why can't an action that is unsuitable for attaining a certain end qualify as "irrational"?
- Why does the objectivity of our science lie in subjectivism?

5. CAUSALITY AS A REQUIREMENT OF ACTION

- In what way does causality influence human action?
- Why is it inevitable, in order to act, to know the causal relationship between events, processes or states of affairs? If a person falsely believes in a causal relationship, can this allow for action?

6. THE ALTER EGO

- How does praxeology deal with the problem of the analysis of other people's actions?
- Why are behaviorism and positivism unsuitable for the explanation of the reality of human action?
- Why are causality and teleology the only appropriate approaches in the field of human research?
- Can praxeology learn anything from animal psychology?
- In what way does praxeology deal with purposeful human action? What distinguishes praxeology from the philosophy of history?

CHAPTER II

THE EPISTEMOLOGICAL PROBLEMS OF THE SCIENCES OF HUMAN ACTION

Chapter Summary

1. PRAXEOLOGY AND HISTORY

Praxeology and history are the two main branches of the sciences of human action. History is the collection and systematic arrangement of all data of experience concerning human action. The natural sciences too deal with past events, but their successful use of induction relies on the experience of past experiments. In contrast, in the sciences of human action there can be no controlled experiment, and hence a different method is needed. Praxeology starts from the fact of human action and uses logical deduction to arrive at a priori truths that are valid for all action, both in the past and future.

2. THE FORMAL AND APRIORISTIC CHARACTER OF PRAXEOLOGY

The logical structure of the human mind is an unanalyzable given. One cannot "prove" logical relations because such a proof itself would rely on logic. The principles of causality (cause and effect) and teleology (i.e., understanding certain events by ascribing conscious motivations) are also necessary prerequisites for the mind to make sense of the world.

11

The Alleged Logical Heterogeneity of Primitive Man

Certain anthropologists believe that the members of primitive tribes possess "prelogical" minds. This confuses the content of their minds with the logical structure. People who do a rain dance are still adopting means to achieve an end; it is simply that they have different technological beliefs from Westerners.

3. THE A PRIORI AND REALITY

Even though praxeology's claims are a priori, they still "teach us" something about reality. Geometrical or mathematical theorems are also "mere" transformations of the initial premises or axioms, yet mathematicians certainly add to human knowledge and allow people to achieve more in the real world.

Far from relying on past experience to generalize and reach a tentative theory of economics, when it comes to human action we can only interpret past exchanges, costs, and so forth with an antecedent knowledge of praxeology. Without knowing beforehand about action, we would only perceive bodily motions, not buying and selling.

4. THE PRINCIPLE OF METHODOLOGICAL INDIVIDUALISM

Praxeology concerns the actions of individuals. It is true that people may behave differently when they view themselves as members of a nation, or when in the midst of an unruly mob. Even so, the "nation" does not bomb another country; individuals in the armed forces choose to obey such orders.

I and We

The collectivist mindset is apparent when people refer to "we" when in fact such individuals had nothing to do with the actions in question. If a U.S. citizen says, "We won World War

Chapter II: The Epistemological Problems of the Sciences of Human Action 13

I," this of course is literally false. There is no such confusion in the term "I."

5. THE PRINCIPLE OF METHODOLOGICAL SINGULARISM

Praxeology deals with individual actions, not vague action in general. Those who think in terms of universals fall into traps such as the classical water-diamond paradox: why is the price of diamonds higher than the price of water, when the latter is more important?

6. THE INDIVIDUAL AND CHANGING FEATURES OF HUMAN ACTION

Although the "common man" doesn't "think for himself," he still chooses to act in the traditional way. If someone votes Republican because her father did, she is still acting in the praxeological sense.

7. THE SCOPE AND THE SPECIFIC METHOD OF HISTORY

The historian can't simply let the facts speak for themselves, because this would lead to a cacophony. Rather he must use his prior value judgments and theories to determine what is relevant and then present the facts accordingly.

The historian can and must rely on the knowledge of other disciplines. But when praxeology, physics, mathematics, etc. cannot contribute anything else to the interpretation of a historical event, the historian relies on understanding, which is his unique contribution.

8. CONCEPTION AND UNDERSTANDING

The task of the sciences of human action is the comprehension of the meaning and relevance of human action. Conception

14   *Study Guide to Human Action*

is the tool of praxeology, while understanding is the tool of history.

Natural History and Human History

The natural sciences too deal with historical events, especially in the fields of cosmology and geology. However, they still rely exclusively on the methods of the natural sciences and do not involve understanding.

9. ON IDEAL TYPES

The historian relies on ideal types that represent his judgments of relevance. Unlike the concepts of praxeology or even the natural sciences, ideal types cannot be described by necessary and sufficient attributes. What economic theory says about "the entrepreneur" is valid for all entrepreneurs, but the historian's use of the term may apply only to a particular period or people.

10. THE PROCEDURE OF ECONOMICS

Economics proceeds with logical deductions from the fact of action. It can study special cases of action by considering specific conditions in which action could occur (for example, if there is a universally accepted medium of exchange).

It would be possible to study the implications of human action in worlds that are utterly different from our own. For example praxeology could consider the case where labor yields no disutility. Yet the end of science is to know reality, and so praxeology restricts its inquiries to those cases where the preconditions could be achieved in the real world. Even so, these deductions are completely a priori. We use our experience to sift out the relevant from the irrelevant chains of thought; we do not use our experience to determine the validity of a particular chain of reasoning.

Chapter II: The Epistemological Problems of the Sciences of Human Action 15

11. THE LIMITATIONS ON PRAXEOLOGICAL CONCEPTS

Praxeology only makes sense when applied to acting human beings. It breaks down into paradox with a being such as the Christian God. Action implies uneasiness, yet an omnipotent being would in one fell swoop achieve perfect contentment.

Why It Matters

Epistemology seeks to answer the question, "How can we ever 'know' something?" In this chapter, Mises establishes the epistemological foundations of praxeology, that is, he explains how it is that economists and other social scientists can arrive at beliefs concerning actors and have confidence in their conclusions.

Especially as the 20th century progressed, most economists thought that they needed to ape the method of the physicists to arrive at "scientific" laws in their field. Mises's insistence that praxeology's propositions are "a priori" thus struck them as shocking and quaint.

If a statement is a priori, its truth can be established without external observations. For example, we can verify the Pythagorean theorem without measuring triangles to "test" the claim. On the other hand, if a statement is a posteriori, then logic alone cannot verify or refute it. For example, if someone says, "the sun emits heat," then sensory observation is necessary to evaluate the claim.

Technical Notes

(1) Mises's taxonomy is a bit confusing. On page 12, he had defined praxeology as the general theory of human action. Yet in the present chapter, on page 30, he refers to praxeology as simply one branch in the "sciences of human action."

(2) Mises claims that the natural sciences advance because of their reliance on experiments, which

> can be used for induction, a peculiar procedure of inference which has given pragmatic evidence of its expediency, although its satisfactory epistemological characterization is still an unsolved problem. (p. 31)

All Mises means here is that philosophers at least since David Hume have noted that there is actually a fallacy involved in the method of the natural sciences. Simply because X led to Y 35 times in a row in the laboratory, does not logically imply that X causes Y. Even so, no one can deny that the experimental method has "worked" in the natural sciences.

(3) Mises distinguishes between a priori and a posteriori statements (see "Why It Matters" above). Hans-Hermann Hoppe draws on Kant to apply yet another distinction, that between analytic and synthetic statements. (Analytic can be determined simply by analyzing the components of the proposition—e.g., "A bachelor is an unmarried

Chapter II: The Epistemological Problems of the Sciences of Human Action 17

male"—while synthetic statements add to our knowledge; they refer to the "real world" and are not merely definitional.) Hoppe argues that Mises's grand achievement was to prove the existence of true, synthetic a priori propositions—something that Hume and other philosophers considered impossible.

Though a fascinating extension of the Misesian framework, it is interesting to note that in *Human Action*, Mises himself never discusses the analytic/synthetic dichotomy.

Study Questions

1. **PRAXEOLOGY AND HISTORY**

   - What are the two main branches of the sciences of human action?

   - What is the field of research of history? Can it tell us something about the future?

   - Is it possible to establish an a posteriori theory of human action with the aid of historical knowledge?

2. **THE FORMAL AND APRIORISTIC CHARACTER OF PRAXEOLOGY**

   - Mises states that the fundamental logical relations are not subject to proof or disproof. Why?

   - What does he mean by methodological apriorism?

   - Why is it fallacious to pretend that the logical structure of the mind of primitive man is different from that of civilized man?

   - Does action imply that it attains the end aimed at?

3. **THE A PRIORI AND REALITY**

   - Can aprioristic reasoning enlarge our knowledge?

Chapter II: The Epistemological Problems of the Sciences of Human Action 19

- Why do the sciences of human action differ radically from the natural sciences?
- Why can't history teach us any general rule, principle, or law?

4. THE PRINCIPLE OF METHODOLOGICAL INDIVIDUALISM

- Can a collective whole act? Why not?
- Why is it necessary to examine collective wholes through an analysis of individuals' actions?
- Why is the acting and choosing being always an Ego?

5. THE PRINCIPLE OF METHODOLOGICAL SINGULARISM

- What does the act of choosing always imply?
- What are the two aspects of every action?

Comment: "A man never chooses between 'gold' and 'iron' in general, but always only between a definite quantity of gold and a definite quantity of iron."

6. THE INDIVIDUAL AND CHANGING FEATURES OF HUMAN ACTION

- How do inheritance and environment direct a man's action?

- How does praxeology deal with routine? Is it due to conscious acting and to a deliberate choice?

7. **THE SCOPE AND THE SPECIFIC METHOD OF HISTORY**

   - Can one present history without any value judgments?
   - What is always the genuine problem of historians?
   - Can history ever refute economic theory?

8. **CONCEPTION AND UNDERSTANDING**

   - What distinguishes the cognition of praxeology from that of history?
   - Can history be scientific?
   - Why can't we measure any constant relations between magnitudes in the field of economics?
   - Why is action always speculation?

9. **ON IDEAL TYPES**

   - Historical facts are unique and unrepeatable. Yet what do they have in common?

   Comment: "[The physicist] transforms the historical event into a fact of the empirical natural sciences. He disregards the active interference of the experimenter and tries to imagine him as an indifferent observer and relater of unadulterated reality."

Chapter II: The Epistemological Problems of the Sciences of Human Action 21

10. THE PROCEDURE OF ECONOMICS

Comment: "[N]o being of human descent that pathological conditions have not reduced to a merely vegetative existence lacks [knowledge of the essence of human action]. No special experience is needed in order to comprehend these theorems, and no experience, however rich, could disclose them to a being who did not know a priori what human action is."

- Because the "end of science is to know reality," what does this imply for the proper procedure of economics?

11. THE LIMITATIONS ON PRAXEOLOGICAL CONCEPTS

- What happened when philosophers and theologians attempted to apply praxeological categories to an absolute being who was not constrained as human actors are?

CHAPTER III

ECONOMICS AND THE REVOLT AGAINST REASON

Chapter Summary

1. THE REVOLT AGAINST REASON

Reason is the primary tool for acting man. The modern revolt against reason was not due to exaggerated claims by the rationalist philosophers. What really happened was that the socialist opponents of the classical economists could not defeat their arguments, and so instead challenged reason itself. Once the floodgates had been opened in this sphere, nihilism and skepticism spilled over into other branches of thought.

2. THE LOGICAL ASPECT OF POLYLOGISM

Marxian polylogism claims that the bourgeois mind operates on different principles from the proletarian mind, while racial polylogism ascribes a different logical structure to the minds of various races. These doctrines fall apart in cases where a worker becomes a factory owner, or parents of different races produce mixed offspring.

It was not enough for the Marxists to dismiss the teachings of Ricardo and other classical economists by referring to their bourgeois minds; to be consistent, Marx and his followers would have had to specify the axioms of proletarian logic versus those of bourgeois logic, and to demonstrate why Ricardian

23

economics was valid in the latter system but not in the former. Obviously no polylogist has ever attempted such a demonstration.

3. THE PRAXEOLOGICAL ASPECT OF POLYLOGISM

Marxists use the term "ideology" to denote a doctrine that is faulty (using the correct, proletarian logic) but which nevertheless serves the interests of a particular class. Such a stance is untenable, though, for how could it ever be in a class's interest to believe false ideas?

Marx developed polylogism in order to discredit the economists' objections to socialism. Rather than refuting their arguments, he simply stated that their doctrines favored the bourgeoisie. Yet psychological motivations, even if base, do not affect the validity of a theory, which either stands or falls on its own merit.

4. RACIAL POLYLOGISM

The claim that different races possess different logical structures of the mind overlooks the fact that reason works. If indeed other races possessed minds that could not grasp cause and effect, or which could not recognize a valid deduction, then natural selection would have weeded out those members who relied on their "minds." To the extent that other organisms have risen above the instinctive behavior of animals, they necessarily must share the (successful) logic enjoyed by the white race.

5. POLYLOGISM AND UNDERSTANDING

A much milder version of polylogism simply asserts that various classes or races share similar value judgments and historical understanding. Yet even this weaker claim ignores the heterogeneity within classes and races. It also repeats the polylogist's

Chapter III: Economics and the Revolt Against Reason   25

mistake of thinking that it can ever be beneficial to hold an erroneous judgment.

6. THE CASE FOR REASON

Reason is an ultimate given, a nonrational fact; one cannot establish the validity of reason itself through logical argument. Yet it is man's foremost tool in action, and distinguishes man from other animals. There can be no such thing as an irrational mode of thinking. To renounce reason and return to guidance by "instinct" would destroy the foundations of civilization.

Why It Matters

Mises considers it crucial to demolish the Marxist notion of polylogism. Without tackling this idea directly, the entire body of praxeology would rest on quicksand. Regardless of the coherence of his demonstrations throughout the rest of the book, the critic could dismiss it all as based on "bourgeois logic."

Technical Notes ·

(1) It is interesting that Mises's handling of Marxian polylogism illustrates his very points on the matter. Mises claims that the motivation for Marx to develop his doctrine was the need to challenge the classical economists (p. 78). Yet Mises's critique doesn't end there. He spends countless pages in *Human Action* detailing the defects of polylogism.

(2) Marxian polylogism is a very strong doctrine and should not be confused with superficially similar attitudes. Mises does not deny that people with different backgrounds may "think differently" about some issues. What he does deny is that such people's minds operate according to different logical structures. Mises also is aware that certain groups can benefit from the perpetuation of faulty beliefs. But the true Marxist doesn't claim that the capitalists financed pamphlets on laissez-faire, knowing full well that the doctrines were wrong. On the contrary, the true Marxist must say that the capitalist mind was incapable of seeing the flaws in the doctrines, because to do so would be detrimental to his interests.

(3) Mises affirms Hoppe's interpretation regarding synthetic a priori truths (though not in these terms) when he writes,

> It is consequently incorrect to assert that aprioristic insight and pure reasoning do not convey any information about reality and the structure of the universe. (p. 86)

Chapter III: Economics and the Revolt Against Reason   27

Study Questions

1. THE REVOLT AGAINST REASON

- What does Mises mean by saying, "The revolt against reason was directed against another target. It did not aim at the natural sciences, but at economics"?

- Why is human reason "constitutionally unfitted" to find truth, according to Marx?

2. THE LOGICAL ASPECT OF POLYLOGISM

- Give examples of some of Mises's "more serious objections" to the concepts of social class and race as applied by the polylogists.

3. THE PRAXEOLOGICAL ASPECT OF POLYLOGISM

- Why is the "ideological" approach erroneous from the praxeological point of view?

- Why is the psychological background of its creator(s) not important for the examination of a theory?

- How does workers' competition among themselves relate to Marx's theory of the interests of the working class?

Comment: "It is ideas that make history, and not history that makes ideas."

4. RACIAL POLYLOGISM

- Why is Marxian polylogism irreconcilable with science and reason?

- Do different races have different logical structures of mind?

- Has anyone ever documented the different logical structures of the minds of people from different races?

5. POLYLOGISM AND UNDERSTANDING

- What determines judgments of value and the choice of ends?

- Who originally said, "You can't make an omelet without breaking eggs"?

6. THE CASE FOR REASON

- Can we study a science of irrationality?

- What drives many intellectuals toward socialism?

- Can we demonstrate the validity of the a priori foundations of logic?

CHAPTER IV

A FIRST ANALYSIS OF THE CATEGORY OF ACTION

Chapter Summary

1. ENDS AND MEANS

The end (or goal or aim) is the result sought by an actor. The means is whatever is used to attain the end. Ends and means do not exist in the physical universe but rather are the product of a valuing mind as it surveys its physical environment.

Praxeology does not concern itself with an idealized actor who has noble ends and knows the best means to achieve any end. On the contrary, praxeology takes an actor's goals and his beliefs on how to satisfy them as the starting point of analysis. If people erroneously believe that a certain root possesses medicinal properties, it will command a price on the market. The economist must take people as they are to explain market phenomena.

The common distinction between free goods and economic goods is unhelpful, for a "free good" isn't scarce and is better classified as a general condition of human well-being. Goods that directly satisfy human wants are consumers' goods or (in Mengerian terminology) goods of the first order. Goods that only satisfy wants indirectly, with the assistance of other goods, are classified as producers' goods, or factors of production, or

29

(following Menger) goods of higher order. One can conceptually arrange the higher-order goods according to their remoteness from the ultimate end; the second-order goods cooperate to yield the first-order (consumer) goods, while the third-order goods are used to produce second-order goods and so forth.

Nonmaterial goods are called services.

2. THE SCALE OF VALUE

An actor has competing ends, but in any given action he must satisfy some wants while leaving others unfulfilled. The praxeologist interprets this behavior by saying that the satisfied end was higher on the scale of value than the others. Value resides not in objects but in the minds of actors who rank those objects as either directly desirable or as means to some other, more ultimate end.

3. THE SCALE OF NEEDS

Although other disciplines (such as physiology) may usefully distinguish between "real" versus "conditioned" or artificial needs, economics has no need of such a scheme. All of economics can be built on the subjective scale of values possessed by actual individuals.

4. ACTION AS AN EXCHANGE

An action is an attempt to substitute a more satisfactory situation for a less desirable one. In this sense, all actions are voluntary exchanges. That which is abandoned is the price of the action, while the costs of the action are the value of the price paid. Another way to express this is to say that the cost of an action is the value placed on satisfaction that must be forgone in order to achieve the chosen end.

Chapter IV: A First Analysis of the Category of Action 31

The difference between the value of the price (i.e., the costs) of an action, and the goal attained, is the gain or profit or net yield of the action. In this sense, profit is a purely subjective category and is immeasurable, for an increase in happiness is a psychic phenomenon that defies quantitative treatment. Actions can only rank ends in an ordinal fashion, i.e., first, second, third, etc. An exchange only demonstrates that which is preferred, not "how much" it is preferred.

Actors are fallible, and often an action will not achieve the end sought. However, if the attained outcome is still preferable to the original situation, then the actor still enjoys a profit (though a smaller one than originally hoped). But if the actual outcome is more unsatisfactory than what was sacrificed in carrying out the action, then the actor suffers a loss.

Why It Matters

This relatively short chapter seems simple enough, but it is truly extraordinary and deserves careful study. For this is where Mises finally links his "philosophical tangents" with "real economics." In particular, Mises shows that the concept of action implies the concepts of value, price, costs, profit, and loss. These are not simply offshoots of an organized market where goods trade against money, but are actually fundamental categories that would exist even for an isolated actor who engages in "barter" with nature.

In this chapter, Mises also lays the framework for the "Austrian" approach to the capital structure, with the hierarchy of goods in terms of their remoteness from the final act of consumption.

Technical Notes

(1) Praxeology neither assumes that people have enlightened value scales, nor that they are omniscient in their pursuit of their aims. This stands in sharp contrast to the approach in mainstream economics, where authors quite explicitly assume that the agents in their models are superhuman calculators capable of solving complex optimization problems.

(2) Mises points out (p. 94) that the purpose of the Mengerian hierarchy of production is purely for conceptual clarity. The economist in practice never needs to determine whether the consumer's good is "really" the loaf of bread at the grocery store, versus the sandwich as it is being lifted to someone's mouth during lunch at home. The important point is that, once an end point is specified (however arbitrarily), all higher-order goods derive their value from the value of that stipulated consumer good.

(3) When Mises writes that the "only source from which our knowledge concerning these [value] scales is derived is the observation of a man's actions" (p. 95), the reader is liable to underestimate the claim. Mises does not simply mean that it is impossible for the outside observer to see another man's value scale, and so must be content to view the man's actions as a proxy. No, Mises believes the much deeper claim that the value

Chapter IV: A First Analysis of the Category of Action

scale is itself a mental construct that only exists in the context of the means-end framework ascribed to an individual. So it is not that the value scale exists and generates an action, but the poor praxeologist can only see the action; rather, Mises claims that the very decision to classify particular physical events as an action implies the notion of a value scale for the identified actor.

(4)   Although it is ambiguous, it appears that Mises may have conceded more to the cardinalists than Rothbard does (e.g., in Rothbard's discussion in "Toward a Reconstruction of Utility and Welfare Economics," where Rothbard criticizes talk of degrees of ordinal rankings, such as a man mildly preferring steak to hamburger but strongly preferring hamburger to rat poison for dinner). When discussing psychic profit, Mises writes,

> There is a more or less in the removal of uneasiness felt; but how much one satisfaction surpasses another one can only be felt; it cannot be established and determined in an objective way. (p. 97)

Indeed it might seem that this concession is necessary, for later on, Mises argues that an action could yield a profit though a "smaller one than that expected" (p. 98). On the face of it, this possibility seems to admit that it is coherent to say that two outcomes are both better than a third, but that one of them is "more better" than the third.

Study Questions

1. ENDS AND MEANS

- What do we call the result sought by an action? What does it relieve?

- What are means? What distinguishes a thing from a means? How can a thing become a means?

- What is economics about?

- Why are means necessarily limited?

- Which goods are objects of human action?

- Which goods are defined as "consumers' goods"?

- Which goods are defined as "producers' goods"?

- Which goods are called services?

2. THE SCALE OF VALUE

- How does the scale of value manifest itself? In praxeology, what is the source of our knowledge concerning an actor's value scale?

Explain: "Value is not intrinsic, it is not in things. It is within us . . ."

Chapter IV: A First Analysis of the Category of Action   35

3. THE SCALE OF NEEDS

- What does action aim at in the first place?

  Explain: "Economics must explain . . . prices . . . as they are, not as they would be under different conditions."

4. ACTION AS AN EXCHANGE

- What is action?

- How is exchange defined?

- What are costs?

- What is profit?

- Why is the cardinal approach erroneous?

- What happens when action doesn't attain the aim sought?

CHAPTER V

TIME

Chapter Summary

1. THE TEMPORAL CHARACTER OF PRAXEOLOGY

In a logical system (such as mathematics) all of the implications are coexistent and interdependent. It is not true that the axioms of geometry "cause" its theorems to be true, even though a limited human mind must work step by step through a geometrical proof.

In the sense that praxeology is a logical system, it too is "out of time." However, the system itself contains parts such as change, causality, and the notions of sooner and later.

Thus the subject matter, the content, of praxeology is intimately related to time.

2. PAST, PRESENT, AND FUTURE

It is action that makes man aware of the flux of time. Time itself is a praxeological category; one can't make sense of time without understanding action, and one can't understand action without the concept of time.

In other disciplines such as philosophy or physics, "the present" is simply an idealized boundary line between the past and the future. But in praxeology, there is a real, extended present.

37

In praxeology, the present is not defined as some unit of duration, measured by clock ticks or revolutions of heavenly bodies. Rather, the present is always defined by the presence of a ripe opportunity to take some potential action. Once the conditions have changed, making a potential action now incapable of achieving its desired end, the "moment has passed" and what was the present is now the past.

3. THE ECONOMIZATION OF TIME

Time is scarce, and as such, it must be economized. This is seen most clearly by considering someone living in a paradise where every material need can be satisfied without any labor. Even in this hypothetical world, people would still need to arrange their satisfactions in a particular temporal sequence. Even though scarcity would not be an issue with regard to goods and services, nonetheless the concepts of *sooner* and *later* would still have meaning.

4. THE TEMPORAL RELATION BETWEEN ACTIONS

Actions (by the same person) can never occur simultaneously, but rather must occur in succession through time. A given action may achieve several ends at once, but it is misleading to classify this as several simultaneous actions.

It is wrong to suppose that a man has a value scale that then "causes" him to act in a certain way. On the contrary, outsiders infer an underlying value scale only to make sense of an action; it is the action that is the brute fact. It is therefore pointless when some thinkers try to judge the actions of individuals with reference to their value scales, as if they could discover some discrepancy or "irrationality."

Chapter V: Time 39

Why It Matters

There are several reasons why this chapter is important. First, time preference is a crucial component of the Misesian theory of interest, and so Mises would naturally want to establish a special role for time in the early chapters when setting up the praxeological framework. Second, Mises wants to demonstrate that the dimension of time is different from the three dimensions of space; Mises uses what O'Driscoll and Rizzo have called Bergsonian time (see footnote 2 on page 100). Unlike space, there is something qualitatively different about time (because of its irreversibility) and this difference has tremendous relevance to action. Finally, this chapter is important because (as we discuss more in the "Technical Notes" below) it underscores the difference between praxeology and mainstream utility theory.

Technical Notes

(1) When Mises writes (p. 99) that "[i]n the frame of the praxeological system any reference to functional correspondence" is misleading and at best metaphorical, his target is mainstream economics. In a neoclassical model, all of the equilibrium values are "simultaneously determined"; it makes no sense to ask, "What causes the price of apples to be $2 per pound?" The honest neoclassical answer to that question is simply, "That's the only price at which the equations will all be true."

(2) Related to the above point is the Misesian emphasis on Bergsonian time (as opposed to mechanical, Newtonian time). Here too, mainstream models illustrate Mises's position through their contrast. In a general equilibrium model as pioneered by Arrow and Debreu, one can certainly deal with "time," but in a very abstract way. For example, one can posit N types of commodities available at any time, and moreover allow the consumer to purchase them in any time periods from t = 1, 2, 3, . . . , T. The nominal gross rate of interest can even be expressed in such a framework as the markup on a particular basket of goods to be delivered at time t rather than time t + 1. Yet clearly this austere approach lacks something; just as a model in classical mechanics, time is simply another dimension and there is nothing peculiar to the future as opposed to the past. In the next

Chapter V: Time 41

chapter, Mises will deal with uncertainty, which is relevant to this difference in viewpoint.

(3) The discussion of consistency (pp. 102–04) again is a reaction to mainstream economics. In formal models of an ordinal value scale, mainstream economists will insist on some "rationality" criteria. For example, they will assume that an agent can compare any two options and determine which one is preferred (or if he is indifferent). They will also usually assume the value scale is transitive, meaning that if a is preferred to b and b is preferred to c, then a is necessarily preferred to c as well. This assumption is necessary in order for mainstream economists to get anywhere with their models; in particular, if they are to employ theorems that show how a cardinal utility function can "represent" an ordinal preference ranking, it is necessary for the ranking to obey transitivity. Mises shows that in the real world, no action could ever demonstrate an intransitive value scale. (In contrast, the "demonstrated preference" approach of Paul Samuelson does allow this possibility, though Samuelson's approach can't work properly in such a case.) Mises would no doubt consider the mainstream preoccupation with value scales to attribute too much to what is really a tool of thought; action is the concrete reality.

Study Questions

1. THE TEMPORAL CHARACTER OF PRAXEOLOGY

- What makes thinking itself an action?

- What distinguishes the logical system from the praxeological system?

2. PAST, PRESENT, AND FUTURE

- Why is action necessarily directed toward the future?

- How does man become conscious of the notion of time?

- What role does the present play for an acting being?

3. THE ECONOMIZATION OF TIME

- What does time have in common with economic goods?

- What distinguishes time from economic goods?

4. THE TEMPORAL RELATION BETWEEN ACTIONS

- What is the meaning of "sooner and later"?

Chapter V: Time
43

- In what way (if any) do yesterday's goals serve today's actions?

- What's wrong with the argument that "if *A* is preferred to *B* and *B* is preferred to *C*, logically *A* is preferred to *C*"?

- What's the difference between the logical concept of consistency and the praxeological concept of consistency?

- How does constancy differ from rationality? Give examples.

- Why does Mises use the example of a speculator at the stock exchange? What is he trying to demonstrate?

CHAPTER VI

UNCERTAINTY

Chapter Summary

1. UNCERTAINTY AND ACTING

Action implies uncertainty of the future. If the future were known, there would be no impetus to action. The praxeologist can recognize this truth without taking a stand on the philosophical question of whether men are really "free." Even if all events really are determined by natural laws, nonetheless we are nowhere near the ability to accurately predict all future events, and hence there is still scope for human action.

2. THE MEANING OF PROBABILITY

The problem of probable inference—that is, of reaching a decision in the face of incomplete knowledge—is a broad one that cuts across many disciplines. However, the formal treatment of probability by the mathematicians has seduced many people into believing they know more than they really do.

There are two totally distinct fields of probability, namely, class and case probability. The former is applicable to the natural sciences and is governed by causality (i.e., mechanical laws of cause and effect), while the latter is applicable to the social

45

sciences and is governed by teleology (i.e., subjective means/ends frameworks).

3. CLASS PROBABILITY

In class probability we know everything about the entire class of events or phenomena, but we know nothing particular about the individuals making up the class. For example, if we roll a fair die we know the entire class of possible outcomes, but we don't know anything about the particular outcome of the next roll—save that it will be an element of the entire class. The formal symbols and operations of the calculus of probability allow the manipulation of this knowledge, but they do not enhance it.

The difference between a gambler and an insurer is not that one uses mathematical techniques. Rather, an insurer must pool the risks by incorporating the entire class (or a reasonable approximation to it). If a life insurance company only sells policies to a handful of people, it is gambling, no matter how sophisticated its actuarial methods.

4. CASE PROBABILITY

Case probability is applicable when we know some of the factors that will affect a particular event, but we are ignorant of other factors that will also influence the outcome.

In case probability, the event in question is not an element of a larger class, of which we have very concrete knowledge. For example, when it comes to the outcome of a particular sporting event or political campaign, past outcomes are informative but do not as such make the situation one of class probability—these types of events form their own "classes."

Other people's actions are examples of case probability. Therefore, even if natural events could be predicted with certainty, it would still be necessary for every actor to be a speculator.

Chapter VI: Uncertainty   47

5. Numerical Evaluation of Case Probability

It is purely metaphorical when people use the language of the calculus of probability in reference to events that fall under case probability. For example, someone can say "I believe there is a 70 percent probability that Hillary Clinton will be the next president."

Yet upon reflection, this statement is simply meaningless. The election in question is a unique event, not a member of a larger class where such frequencies could be established.

6. Betting, Gambling, and Playing Games

When a man risks money on an outcome where he knows some of the factors involved, he is betting. When he risks money on an outcome where he knows only the frequencies of the various elements of the class, he is gambling. (The two activities roughly match up with the case/class probability distinction.) To play a game is a special type of action, though the reverse is not true; not all actions can be usefully described as part of a game.

In particular, the attempt to model the market economy with "game theory" is very misleading, because in (most) games the participants try to beat their opponents, while in a market all participants benefit.

7. Praxeological Prediction

Praxeology can make certain predictions about the future, but they are necessarily qualitative. For example, it can tell us that (other things equal) a fall in the demand for apples will lead to a lower price of apples. But praxeology alone can never tell us that (say) a particular change will yield a 9 percent drop in apple prices. Such quantitative forecasts are possible with the aid of understanding, but then of course they are no longer certain.

Why It Matters

In this short chapter, Mises accomplishes several things. First, he establishes the necessary connection between action and uncertainty. Inasmuch as neoclassical economics ignored uncertainty for many decades, this alone is important. But beyond that, Mises shows the limitations of formal mathematical approaches to probability. This has continuing relevance because the mainstream economists answered the criticisms of "perfect information" by simply pushing the problem back one step; instead of assuming that the agents in their models knew the future perfectly, they assumed that their agents knew the exact probability distributions of random variables in the models, which in turn would determine future outcomes. (Israel Kirzner has written extensively on this nonsolution to the problem.) For a third contribution, Mises nonchalantly offers a brilliant approach to defining class probability itself, and as an aside points out the circularity in conventional mathematical treatments!

Technical Notes

(1) Here (pp. 106–07) and elsewhere in the book, Mises refers to the "theorems" of the natural sciences. This usage differs from how most scientists would talk in modern times. In current usage, a theorem is a deductively proven result. In context it is clear that Mises is discussing what the physicists and chemists themselves would classify as theories.

(2) In discussing class probability, Mises refers to the "crude circularity implied in all definitions referring to the equiprobability of possible events" (p. 109). What he seems to have in mind is the typical approach to probability in some mathematical texts, where (say) the definition of a 1/2 probability is "the likelihood of an outcome when it and one other outcome are equally likely." This approach is circular, because it defines the concept of probability with reference to the concept of probability.

(3) Modern economists might scoff at Mises's curt dismissal of game theory (pp. 116–17). In particular, they might argue that game theory can model situations in which all players benefit from cooperation. At the time of Mises's writing, however, von Neumann and Morgenstern's pioneering treatise (see p. 117, n. 3) was only a few years old, and in this work game theory was still focused on "zero-sum" games, i.e., games where

one player's gain was another's loss. Moreover, this is what most people mean by the term "game." Modern game theory has indeed moved beyond this restriction, but only by broadening the term to include any strategic interaction where one player's payoff is a function not only of his own actions but of all other players' actions as well.

Chapter VI: Uncertainty   *51*

Study Questions

1. **UNCERTAINTY AND ACTING**

   - What is the role of uncertainty in the field of action?

   - Are actions always risky? Why?

2. **THE MEANING OF PROBABILITY**

   Comment: "The treatment of probability has been confused by the mathematicians."

   - Why did John Stuart Mill use the term "the real opprobrium of mathematics" in reference to the calculus of probability?

3. **CLASS PROBABILITY**

   - What is the definition of class probability?

   - What supplementary information can we get from the calculus of probability?

   - How does the insurance business differ from gambling?

   - Does insurance belong to the field of class probability? Why?

4. **CASE PROBABILITY**

   - What is the definition of case probability?

- What are the main differences between case probability and class probability?

- What are the differences between luck, gambling, speculation, and risk?

5. NUMERICAL EVALUATION OF CASE PROBABILITY

- Why isn't case probability open to numerical evaluation?

- Why is understanding important for problems of case probability?

6. BETTING, GAMBLING, AND PLAYING GAMES

- What are the differences between betting and gambling? How does gambling become betting?

- Is betting an action? Is gambling an action?

- Why do psychologists have a tendency to confuse combat and competition?

- Why is it inappropriate to use military terms for the description of business operations?

7. PRAXEOLOGICAL PREDICTION

- What can be predicted with the aid of praxeological knowledge?

- What distinguishes quantitative approaches from qualitative ones?

CHAPTER VII

ACTION WITHIN THE WORLD

Chapter Summary

1. THE LAW OF MARGINAL UTILITY

Acting man must place all ends onto a single scale of values. If he is to choose between (say) acquiring a steak or attending the opera, he must decide which outcome yields the most utility, and thus these entirely different satisfactions must be compared according to a common denominator. Even so, action doesn't measure utility; rather, it is action that demonstrates the end most highly valued by the actor.

Even though all satisfactions are ultimately placed on a single scale of values, it is still useful to classify various means in groups that yield identical results, i.e., to classify means as units of particular goods. Note that even though successive units of a means (by definition) yield identical results, the utility of these results is not identical. Indeed, the utility of successive units of a given good decreases, because the actor will apply the additional units to ends deemed less and less urgent.

The law of decreasing marginal utility is not a physiological or psychological one, but is rooted in the very fact of action. An actor will always devote a given stock of means to attaining the highest state of satisfaction, and that is why additional units of a good will be devoted to less and less important ends (and hence will have lower marginal utility).

Marginal utility is always defined according to the subjective framework of the actor in question. The relevant "margin" is determined by the choice, not physical or otherwise "objective" constraints. There are no arithmetical operations possible with the utility ascribed to various units. It is possible that the marginal unit of water is far less valuable than the marginal unit of diamonds, even though the utility of the entire stock of water is far more valuable. Yet this latter fact is irrelevant to action, since no one is ever in the position of choosing between all the water and all the diamonds.

2. THE LAW OF RETURNS

Even though all satisfactions are ultimately ranked on an ordinal scale—which is not subject to cardinal manipulation—it is still crucial for an actor to understand the quantitative causal relations of the world. When it comes to a consumer good, each unit yields the same quantity of effect; this is how the units are defined, after all. (Of course successive doses of this same quantity of effect have lower and lower utility.)

Things are more complicated when it comes to producer goods. Here a given unit of a producer good must always act in combination with at least one other producer good in order to yield a definite quantity of a consumer good. (If the higher-order good could yield the first-order good by itself with no reliance on other scarce inputs, then it would itself be a first-order good.)

With full understanding of the technological processes involved, one can compute the additional yield of output attributable to successive units of input of a particular producer good, holding the quantity of all other inputs fixed. At some finite

Chapter VII: Action Within the World 55

point, an "optimum" level will be reached, in the sense that the quantity of output per unit of input (of the producer good that is being varied) is maximized. Economists often describe this as the point at which "diminishing returns" set in, meaning that further increases in the input result in proportionally smaller increases in output. The notion of diminishing returns explains why farmers must bring additional land under cultivation, rather than continually pumping more fertilizer and seeds into a given plot of land.

3. HUMAN LABOR AS A MEANS

The employment of the powers of the human body as a means is labor. As a general rule, labor carries disutility. That is, even though actors deploy the entire available stock of other means in order to achieve the highest satisfaction, they will not devote the physiological-maximum amount of labor to achieve attainable ends. On the contrary, they will refrain from possible labor in order to enjoy leisure. The economist can handle this empirical fact by acknowledging that (in this world) human actors value leisure as a consumer good. As an actor works additional hours, the disutility of labor increases because the marginal utility of the good leisure is continually rising (as the supply of leisure shrinks). At some point (usually well before the physiological maximum) the marginal utility of the physical fruits of an additional unit of labor is lower than the marginal disutility of an additional unit of labor; at this point the actor ceases to labor.

Everything that is true of a generic factor of production is hence true of labor. However, labor still receives special consideration from the economist because labor is the ultimate "nonspecific" factor; labor is required in every production process. Moreover, in our world labor is the scarcest of inputs. In a market economy with flexible wage rates, all willing laborers are channeled to those ends deemed most urgent; there is no analog to land that remains uncultivated.

Immediately Gratifying Labor and Mediately Gratifying Labor

Although many writers have misunderstood this fact, it is true that some workers derive pleasure from (usually small) applications of labor. Even so, it is still true that the vast majority of labor expended in our world involves disutility, and that no social reform can elude the fact that humans will, as a rule, choose to engage in labor past the point at which it is immediately gratifying (because they value the output more than the forfeited leisure).

The Creative Genius

Mises believes that the "output" of the creative genius cannot usefully be treated in the same framework that praxeology uses for the work of other laborers. Mises believes that a creative genius "labors" neither for immediate nor mediate gratification.

4. PRODUCTION

Production is not creative; it rather transforms the given material objects of the universe into forms that are more pleasing to actors. The true creation occurs in the mind of the actor, who surveys the available means and conceives of a way to improve his condition.

Early economists classified the labor of farmers and carpenters as "productive," while those of doctors and singers as "unproductive," because of the intangible and fleeting character of the services of the latter. Modern economists laugh at such irrelevant distinctions, yet they themselves often consider advertising as "wasteful."

Chapter VII: Action Within the World 57

Why It Matters

Mises spends most of his time in section 1 guarding against the numerous fallacies and misconceptions regarding marginal utility. Mainstream economists often treated utility as a cardinal substance that could be manipulated mathematically; the utility of a stock of goods was seen as the integral of the utility of each infinitesimal unit. Other writers tried to explain decreasing marginal utility as an empirical regularity, and they pointed to the Weber-Fechner law, which demonstrated, e.g., that people need larger and larger increments of intensity in order to distinguish between brighter and brighter lights. Yet as Mises points out, the law of decreasing marginal utility is applicable to any actor, whether or not he (or it) has a body with sensory organs that operate like the typical human's.

Mises accomplishes a great deal in the space devoted to labor. He first defines labor, and explains why it deserves special treatment from the modern economist. Having said that, he explodes numerous fallacies regarding labor and how it is allegedly different from other factors of production.

Technical Notes

(1)   Not only is the utility of the marginal unit sub-
      jective, but the definition of the unit itself
      depends on the actor and the circumstances. For
      example, a chemist might determine that one
      carton of milk contains 1.01 gallons while
      another contains 0.99 gallons, yet the consumer
      could quite properly consider them interchange-
      able "units of milk," each yielding the same
      objective services.

(2)   Mises says that the "optimum" amount of input is
      the one that maximizes the output per unit of
      input (p. 127). Of course in this context "opti-
      mum" is a technological description; an actor
      might attain the highest utility by operating above
      or below this technologically "optimum" level.
      Also, note that the optimum level—which Mises
      says maximizes output per unit of input—is not
      the level that maximizes the marginal physical
      yield of the input good. (Generally speaking, the
      marginal physical yield will reach its maximum
      before Mises's "optimum" level is reached, and for
      some range above this amount of input the aver-
      age physical yield will still rise. When the falling
      marginal yield "crosses" the average yield, Mises's
      "optimum" level is reached and then both will
      begin to fall as the declining marginal yield "pulls
      down" the average yield.)

Chapter VII: Action Within the World   59

(3)   Many Austrians disagree with Mises (pp. 138–40)
       that the creative genius cannot be handled within
       the framework of praxeology. It may be true that
       the genius does not labor for his fellow men or
       even for his "output," but, even so, he acts (in
       composing a play, a symphony, etc.) in order to
       remove felt uneasiness. The fact that a creative
       genius may never reveal his potential if placed in
       adverse circumstances proves that his creation is a
       choice and not a mere datum of the environment
       to which acting men must adapt.

Study Questions

1. UNCERTAINTY AND ACTING

- Action can only be expressed by ordinal numbers. But how are quantitative facts involved?
- What implies choice from a praxeological point of view?
- Given the following value scale:

    1. *a* (first unit)
    2. *a* (second unit)
    3. *b* (first unit)
    4. *a* (third unit)
    5. *b* (second unit)
    6. *b* (third unit)
    7. *a* (fourth unit)
    8. *a* (fifth unit)
    9. *b* (fourth unit)

    - If the actor possesses the 9 items shown, will he prefer to lose 2 units of *a* or 1 unit of *b*?

    - If the actor already possesses 3 units of *a* and 3 units of *b*, will he prefer 1 additional unit of *a* or 1 additional unit of *b*?

    - If the actor must choose between all 5 units of *a* versus all 4 units of *b*, can we say which he will select?

Chapter VII: Action Within the World 61

- What is the definition of utility?

- What distinguishes subjective use-value from objective use-value?

- How was it possible to solve the value paradox? Who solved the problem?

- Are prices derived from subjective use-value?

- Is "total utility" relevant for praxeology?

- What can marginal utility explain that total utility can't?

- Does praxeology have a need for the notion of a "class of wants"?

- Why can't we compare valuations of different people?

- What are the flaws in Bernoulli's approach to the law of diminishing marginal utility?

2. THE LAW OF RETURNS

- Why isn't a recipe considered an economic good?

- What is the definition of the law of returns? Can we say that it is a priori true?

- Which problems can't be solved with the help of the law of returns?

3. HUMAN LABOR AS A MEANS

- Why is labor not an end in itself? Is labor an economic good?

- What is the relation between work and leisure? Why is work linked to disutility?

- Is leisure an economic good? Can we apply the principle of marginal utility?

- How can we explain the tendency toward the reduction of working hours?

- What does "nonspecific character" mean in connection with human labor?

- Why can a shortage of specialists only emerge in the short run, according to Mises?

- In what conditions could there be an abundance of labor?

- Is labor more scarce than material factors of production? What does it mean for a market society?

- Are geniuses substitutable?

4. PRODUCTION

Comment: "Man is creative only in thinking and in the realm of imagination."

- How is it erroneous to make a distinction between the employment of labor and that of material factors of production?

- Why is production an intellectual phenomenon that is guided by human reason?

Part Two—Action Within the Framework of Society

CHAPTER VIII

HUMAN SOCIETY

Chapter Summary

1. HUMAN COOPERATION

Society is the combination of individuals for cooperative effort. People collaborate—form social bonds—because they perceive the greater productivity afforded by the division of labor. This doesn't mean that people set about to "form" society, but rather that each particular act of cooperation was the outcome of deliberation. The feelings of belonging and camaraderie that characterize society are an offshoot of the material advantages of the division of labor. Without the latter, mere sentiments would not be sufficient to hold society together.

2. A CRITIQUE OF THE HOLISTIC AND METAPHYSICAL VIEW OF SOCIETY

Throughout history many religious and other metaphysical intellectuals argued that society had an existence independent of the individuals composing it. God, Nature, or some other force had His or its own ends for society, and the shortsighted and wicked individuals had to be forced to sacrifice their own selfish interests in order to achieve the greater plan.

63

The classical economists demonstrated that such theories are unnecessary. Social cooperation serves the interests of everyone; virtually all people prefer the advantages of civilization to the fleeting thrill of murder, theft, and other antisocial behavior.

Although society serves the rightly understood interests of all people, nonetheless some individuals are too narrow-minded or lack the moral will to respect the rules of civilized behavior. Mises believes that the function of a state or government is to check the antisocial behavior of such people.

Because all governments, no matter how despotic, ultimately rest on the tacit consent of the people, classical liberalism supports democracy as the only way to maintain peace. In other words, because the majority are going to get the rulers they want in any event, classical liberalism suggests ballots rather than bullets. This endorsement of democracy is purely to minimize violence, and doesn't rest on a naïve faith in the wisdom of the common man.

Praxeology and Liberalism

Liberalism is a political doctrine. In praxeology, "happiness" and "satisfaction" are purely formal terms. Yet in liberalism they take on concrete form; it is assumed that all (or most) men prefer wealth to poverty and health to sickness. Liberalism relies on the value-free theorems of praxeology in order to recommend the best routes to achieving these nearly universally held values.

Liberalism and Religion

Liberalism is a rational political doctrine that does not itself refer to God or other supernatural elements. However, it is wrong to view liberalism as "atheistic." On the contrary, the separation of church and state—a hallmark of liberalism—

Chapter VIII: Human Society 65

allows the various sects to preach their views unmolested. Liberalism certainly opposes theocracy, but not religion per se.

3. THE DIVISION OF LABOR

The superiority of the division of labor means that the yield per hour of labor can be increased when workers act in cooperation with each other. This empirical phenomenon is due to (1) the innate inequality of the abilities of workers in various tasks, (2) the unequal distribution of resources on the surface of the earth, and (3) the fact that some tasks are beyond the power of a single worker.

4. THE RICARDIAN LAW OF ASSOCIATION

David Ricardo is credited with the discovery of the law of association, or the law of comparative cost. Although it is obvious that cooperation can make two people better off when each is the superior producer of a particular good, Ricardo took the argument a step further. Even if one person is superior at producing everything, even so he benefits from cooperating with the inferior partner. For example, a master chef benefits from hiring subordinates to chop vegetables and prepare the other ingredients, even if the chef could have performed these tasks better than the employees. This is because "outsourcing" the tasks to the inferior workers frees up the chef's time and allows him to concentrate on those areas in which his advantage is greatest.

Current Errors Concerning the Law of Association

Ricardo's demonstration makes some strong assumptions, for example that there are only two countries producing two goods, and that capital and labor are immobile within each country. However, his argument illustrates a central proposition of economics. The fact that even superior individuals can benefit from cooperation with "inferior" peers is the basis of civilization.

5. The Effects of the Division of Labor

The innate differences between men and regions of the world both cause and are enhanced by the division of labor. The introduction of mechanical, "labor saving" devices was only possible once the division of labor had transformed complicated projects into a succession of smaller tasks.

6. The Individual Within Society

Man emerged as a social being. There was never a time when (what we would call) humans lived in an asocial way. Praxeology deals with the isolated individual but that is only to understand his action.

The Fable of the Mystic Communion

The various theories of social bonds founder if they do not acknowledge the primacy of the division of labor.

7. The Great Society

Not all interhuman relations are social; war is of course antisocial. However, even here the recognition of the division of labor led to the gradual reduction in severity of hostilities. Conquerors no longer slaughtered their vanquished foes outright, but instead enslaved them. The development of "rules" of civilized warfare carried the process further.

8. The Instinct of Aggression and Destruction

Some writers extol the manly urges to kill and destroy that have allegedly been sapped by "unnatural" modern society. It

Chapter VIII: Human Society   *67*

may very well be that people thirst for bloodshed, but they also hunger for food and pang for fancy houses. Praxeology teaches that people must choose between these satisfactions.

Current Misinterpretations of Modern Natural Science, Especially of Darwinism

Modern liberalism does not rely on the (false) belief that men are created equal. Darwinism does not in any way invalidate the liberal creed; on the contrary, the traits conducive to social cooperation (rather than the allegedly "natural" instincts of aggression) are precisely those that maximize one's offspring in the current environment. Far from being unnatural, reason is the foremost biological mark of *homo sapiens*.

Why It Matters

In this chapter, Mises aims to do nothing less than establish the foundation of civilization. Society is the great means through which individuals enhance their own productivity and thus attain a far greater state of satisfaction than would be possible in isolation. However, social bonds can only develop in an environment of peace and respect for property. Because the majority will always achieve what they desire (through force if necessary), the only hope for civilization is to persuade the masses that social cooperation is in their own interest.

Technical Notes

(1)   People often ask, "Was Mises an anarchist?" As the discussion on pages 148–49 makes clear, the immediate answer is no. However, a closer reading shows that Mises here uses anarchism to mean a lack of law enforcement. Nowhere does Mises discuss why the state must provide law, police, and military defense. He simply assumes that these are the proper functions of the state, and since they are necessary for society, therefore (Mises argues) the state is necessary.

(2)   Mises (pp. 161–62) underscores that the Ricardian law of association doesn't rely on the (fallacious) classical theory of value. Because of his restrictive assumptions, Ricardo's analysis could be couched purely in physical terms and he was thus able to provide a useful theorem even without the benefit of the modern subjective theory of value. If one wishes to go beyond the limitations of Ricardo's demonstration, the only recourse is to analyze in terms of money.

Chapter VIII: Human Society 69

Study Questions

1. HUMAN COOPERATION

- What is society?

Comment: "[S]ociety is nothing but the combination of individuals for cooperative effort."

- Can society act?

- Why did cooperation and society emerge, according to Mises? What role does the division of labor play?

2. A CRITIQUE OF THE HOLISTIC AND METAPHYSICAL VIEW OF SOCIETY

- Why and under which conditions does an individual substitute concerted action for isolated action? How is this opposed to the holistic doctrines?

- Why is society a product of human action?

- Has society been designed by humans?

- What is the essential problem of all the variants of collectivist ideas?

- What is Mises's perception of anarchism?

- What is the role of democracy, according to Mises? What does he think about majorities?

- In what way does his definition of the state differ from that of the socialists?

Comment: "[Liberalism] has full confidence in man's reason. It may be that this optimism is unfounded and that the liberals have erred. But then there is no hope left for mankind's future."

3. THE DIVISION OF LABOR

- Why is the division of labor more productive than isolated subsistence?

4. THE RICARDIAN LAW OF ASSOCIATION

- What does the law of association show with regard to the division of labor?

- Consider the following example (note that Sally is more productive in both lines):

	1 Unit of p	1 Unit of q
Joe	3 hours	2 hours
Sally	2 hours	1 hour

If Joe and Sally each give 60 hours to producing p and 60 hours to producing q, what would each get to consume in isolation? Is there a way they could cooperate so that (with the same expenditure of 120 hours each) they each consumed more of both goods than was possible without trade? (Hint: Suppose that Joe specializes entirely in the production of good p.)

*Chapter VIII: Human Society*71

- What is the difference between the law of association and the law of comparative cost?

- How does the law of association relate to free trade?

- How does the mobility of factors of production affect Ricardo's law?

5. **THE EFFECTS OF THE DIVISION OF LABOR**

- Why does the division of labor intensify the innate inequality of men?

6. **THE INDIVIDUAL WITHIN SOCIETY**

- What is the natural state of man?

- Why is it romantic nonsense to praise the days of primitive barbarism?

Comment: "The mystical experience of communion or community is not the source of societal relations, but their product."

7. **THE GREAT SOCIETY**

- Why is peace preferable to war?

- What does society always imply with regard to human interactions?

8. **THE INSTINCT OF AGGRESSION AND DESTRUCTION**

- What is meant by "social Darwinism"? Is the term still used today?

- What distinguishes man from other animals?

- How did utilitarians show that cooperation is beneficial for the "most efficient" and the "less efficient"?

- Why do utilitarians recommend equality under the civil law?

CHAPTER IX

THE ROLE OF IDEAS

Chapter Summary

1. HUMAN REASON

Reason distinguishes man from other animals. All action is preceded by thinking. The reasoning employed may be faulty, but, by definition, action is the purposeful attempt to remove uneasiness. It is always an individual, not "society," who thinks. Tradition—primarily through language—allows present actors to incorporate into their own thinking the reasoning of their ancestors. This renders present thinking more productive, just as labor is now more productive because of our inheritance of capital goods created by our forefathers.

2. WORLDVIEW AND IDEOLOGY

A worldview serves as both an interpretation of all things, but also as a guide to action. In this sense a worldview is both an explanation and a technology. Ideology is a narrower term, in that it restricts attention to human interaction over earthly concerns. Religious dogma and even the pure natural sciences thus fall outside the scope of ideology.

Even though the various ideologies are, on the surface, quite incompatible, they all champion the same things for their followers. Every party promises to deliver economic prosperity, (eventual) peace, a reduction in disease, and so forth. Thus their disagreements are not over abstract principles on which compromise is impossible. In contrast to truly religious wars, when it comes to secular (i.e., ideological) conflict there is hope for cooperation, because human society is the great means by which all people can better achieve their differing objectives.

The Fight Against Error

A popular view holds that an ideology is most successful when it contains contradictory tenets, because after all "life isn't logical." This is completely false. Reason is man's primary tool in the struggle against nature, and it does no good to let action be guided by contradictory beliefs. In this case the action will be in vain, and worse the contradictory belief system may make it difficult to understand why.

The tendency to denounce adherents to rival ideologies as evil or insane is deplorable. Ironically, the allegedly "paranoid" monetary cranks and even Nazi theorists were simply more consistent in applying the principles of commonly held views regarding the benefits of government intervention in the economy.

3. MIGHT

Human action creates society, and human action is guided by ideology. In this sense, society is a product of ideology. The Marxists therefore have things exactly backwards, since they assert that the material forces of the social order condition the ideology of the day.

Might is the power to direct the actions of others. Rule is the exercise of might in the political arena. Even though a ruler relies on violence to punish dissenters, it is ultimately ideology rather than guns that keeps a particular person or party in power. Without a group who voluntarily obey his orders, the tyrant would be

Chapter IX: The Role of Ideas 75

a lone individual who at most could harm a few dozen people. In this loose sense, all governments rest on popular opinion.

Traditionalism as an Ideology

Traditionalism is an ideology that considers good and expedient the value judgments, customs, and procedures handed down from ancestors. Often the "traditional" doctrines are not really the ones held by ancestors.

4. MELIORISM AND THE IDEA OF PROGRESS

The notions of progress and retrogression only make sense in the context of an actor's plan. Evolution in the biological sense is purposeless and hence it is impermissible to view creatures as gradually improving over time and turning into "higher" forms of life.

The fatal flaw of 18th- and 19th-century rationalists and (classical) liberals was their faith in the decency and wisdom of the common man. These reformers attributed the barbarism of human history to the political power of the aristocrats and kings. Since democracy allowed the direct rule of the many, these enlightened thinkers considered social progress inevitable. What they failed to predict was that the masses were quite fallible and could fall sway to horrible ideologies.

Why It Matters

In previous chapters, Mises made the case for reason, a single system of logic for the human mind, and so forth. In the present chapter, Mises argues that ideas control human destiny. Thus, not only is it sensible to discuss ideas and their relative merits; it is vital to do so because civilization depends on them.

Technical Notes

(1) The Marxists believe that ideologies (except Marxism of course) are simply adapted to justify the economic and social order of a given period. For example, once the material conditions of production rendered feudalism unsustainable, modern capitalism burst onto the scene. In the wake of this "real" transformation, the intangible moral, legal, and political superstructures had to change in order to maintain the rule of the capitalists, the new oppressors of the proletariat. Mises, of course, believes just the opposite, namely, that the Industrial Revolution could not occur until political and legal reforms gave the people of Western Europe a degree of autonomy from their rulers.

(2) When Mises writes (p. 192) that one must guard against the incorporation of the idea of progress in biological evolution, he is limiting himself to the scope of what the natural sciences can teach us. The accepted modern statement of Darwinian theory holds that it is a naïve confusion to view evolution as a billion-year process in which *homo sapiens* are eventually reached. Without positing an actor (such as God) who designed the process, there is no goal and hence the term "progress" is inapplicable. In the present day, bacteria can certainly thrive in many areas of the planet, and so (from a purely biological viewpoint) there is no sense in which humans are more "evolved" than the bacteria are.

Chapter IX: The Role of Ideas

Study Questions

1. **HUMAN REASON**

   - What is the relation between thinking and action?

   - Why is it always the individual who thinks?

   - What is language? Why is it important?

   - What stimulates intellectual progress?

2. **WORLDVIEW AND IDEOLOGY**

   - What are the differences between worldview and ideology?

   - Why is it fallacious to believe that one group can only prosper at the expense of other groups?

   - What is the definition of a party?

   Comment: "The main objective of praxeology and economics is to substitute consistent correct ideologies for the contradictory tenets of popular eclecticism."

   - What is a monetary crank?

   - How can we fight error?

3. **MIGHT**

   - What is might?

- To what does someone owe his might?

- What is the difference between a government that uses violent oppression and a gangster who overpowers a weaker person?

- Can minority rule endure?

4. MELIORISM AND THE IDEA OF PROGRESS

- What are the definitions of progress and retrogression?

- Men err very often. How is this compatible with democracy?

Comment: "There is but one yardstick for the appraisal of human action: whether or not it is fit to attain the ends aimed at by acting men."

CHAPTER X

EXCHANGE WITHIN SOCIETY

Chapter Summary

1. AUTISTIC EXCHANGE AND INTERPERSONAL EXCHANGE

All action is an exchange, of giving up what is less satisfactory for (the actor hopes) what is more satisfactory. Autistic exchange concerns only one actor, while interpersonal exchange involves cooperation between two or more individuals. Although the emergence of social cooperation occurred gradually in the course of history, the conceptual line between autistic versus interpersonal exchange is sharp.

2. CONTRACTUAL BONDS AND HEGEMONIC BONDS

People can cooperate either in a contractual or in a hegemonic relationship. In the former, the participants are on an equal footing. In the latter, one person or group is in charge over the subordinates. Even in a hegemonic structure, the subordinate still acts. He simply chooses subjection over the alternative.

The achievements of modern civilization are the result of contractual bonds. The modern state is a hegemonic structure, though some nations enjoy the "rule of law" (i.e., strict and known limits to the sovereign's power) to a greater extent than others. Contractual societies can live in peace, while hegemonic ones cannot coexist because each hegemon will desire to incorporate autonomous neighbors under his rule.

3. CALCULATIVE ACTION

All action uses ordinal numbers, in the sense that possible outcomes must be ranked on the scale of values to determine which action will result in the highest possible satisfaction. The use of cardinal numbers in action requires special conditions. It was in the context of a contractual society that the use of arithmetic as an aid to action developed.

The distinction between calculable and noncalculable action is of the utmost importance. Modern civilization is possible only because people have learned how to apply arithmetic to so many different fields. Economics itself may be described as a theory of that scope of human action that relies on calculation.

Why It Matters

This short chapter provides the link between Part II ("Action Within the Framework of Society") and Part III ("Economic Calculation") of the book. As the book progresses, its scope narrows. Part I focused on human action and thus exchange per se, while Part II dealt with interpersonal exchange. Part III refines the study to interpersonal exchange when calculation is possible, and thus marks the beginning of economics proper in *Human Action*.

Chapter X: Exchange Within Society

Technical Notes

(1)   Mises's discussion of hegemonic relations (pp. 196–99) is quite nuanced, and the modern Austro-libertarian reader should take care in reading this section. Mises does not seem to be merely distinguishing aggression from nonaggression. For example, he classifies the family as a hegemonic institution. He also says that

> in a hegemonic body a man neither gives nor receives anything that is definite. He integrates himself into a system in which he has to render indefinite services and will receive what the director is willing to assign to him. . . . He is at the mercy of the director. The director alone is free to choose.

One can certainly imagine socialists using these words as a description of (at least some) types of "wage slavery," in which the workers only choose at the outset to work for a particular employer, but after that are completely subject to the commands of the boss. The immediate retort, namely, that the worker under capitalism can always quit, is also true in a hegemonic relation: at any moment the subordinate may choose to renounce his subjection and openly defy the hegemon.

(2)   When Mises discusses calculation (p. 200), he continually uses the word arithmetic rather than mathematics. These terms are not interchangeable, and

Mises is properly choosing arithmetic. When he writes that no other distinction is more important than that between calculable and noncalculable action, he doesn't have in mind (say) that engineers couldn't build bridges without knowledge of geometry. No, Mises is making the much more fundamental point that what we know of as "economy" would be impossible if shepherds couldn't number their flocks or merchants couldn't compare different potential trades to see which offered the best price.

Chapter X: Exchange Within Society

Study Questions

1. AUTISTIC EXCHANGE AND INTERPERSONAL EXCHANGE

- What is the difference between an autistic and an interpersonal exchange?

- Is exchange a win-win situation?

2. CONTRACTUAL BONDS AND HEGEMONIC BONDS

- Why does a contract imply mutuality?

- Does a state imply hegemonic organization?

- In what way did contractual relations help to form human civilization?

- What distinguishes a *Rechtsstaat* from a *Wohl - fahrtsstaat*?

3. CALCULATIVE ACTION

- What is the relationship between action and nonaction?

Explain: "No other distinction is of greater significance, both for human life and for the study of human action, than that between calculable action and noncalculable action."

- Why is economic calculation so fundamental?

Part Three—Economic Calculation

CHAPTER XI

VALUATION WITHOUT CALCULATION

Chapter Summary

1. THE GRADATION OF THE MEANS

Acting man values means according to the valuation he places on the ends they can achieve. (An apple seed is valued through consideration of the future apples it can produce for consumption.) The totality of means needed for a given end would possess the same value as the end, except for the discount due to the waiting time involved. (The concept of time preference will be discussed in a later chapter.)

Often actors must choose between various outcomes that all consist of countable supplies of different goods. Even so, the fundamental act of choice always involves a purely ordinal value judgment, not a quantitative "measurement" of subjective value. If a person, in one fell swoop, trades away five oranges in exchange for eight apples, all we can conclude is that he derived more satisfaction from "eight apples" than from "five oranges." The units involved allow us to go no further than if he had traded away one baseball card for one lollipop.

85

2. THE BARTER-FICTION OF THE ELEMENTARY THEORY OF VALUE AND PRICES

The modern theory of economic value traces back the objective, quantitative prices in a market economy to the subjective, ordinal rankings of individual actors. In such an exposition "imaginary constructions" are needed, i.e., the economist must rely on simplifications in order to analyze one part of the economy, even though in the real world such a simplification would disrupt the very element being analyzed.

In this chapter, Mises discusses the imaginary construction of the barter economy, i.e., the tentative (and false) assumption that all exchange ratios emerge with goods being traded directly against each other, with no use for a medium of exchange (i.e., money) at all.

This assumption is necessary to understand the actual role of money. However, historically it led many economists into two great errors. First, many economists believed that money was neutral and served only to facilitate the "real" transactions that had been studied in the imagined state of barter. So if, say, the economist concluded that, in barter, one apple traded for two oranges, then it was a mere afterthought to add in money and conclude that (say) one apple traded for $1 and one orange traded for 50 cents.

The second great error of many economists was to suppose that items exchanged in a market were of equal value. Even the great classical economists thought that long-run prices were due to the quantity of labor needed to produce the goods in question. The modern subjective theory of value starts with the realization that people trade goods precisely because they value them differently. When Joe gives up his apple for Mary's orange, this doesn't prove that each fruit has equal value. On the contrary, it shows that Joe values the orange more than the apple, while Mary values the apple more than the orange.

Chapter XI: Valuation Without Calculation　　　　　*87*

The Theory of Value and Socialism

The socialists, Institutionalists, and Historical School attack the economists' attention to the problems of the isolated individual, commonly referred to as "Crusoe economics." Although it is necessary to first understand autarkic exchange before proceeding to interpersonal exchange, nonetheless there is some validity in the charge. Ironically, the Crusoe approach is inadequate because it cannot illustrate economic calculation, which is what vitiates the entire program of the socialists and other critics of the economists.

3. THE PROBLEM OF ECONOMIC CALCULATION

Technology is quantitative; it tells actors how many units of various inputs are necessary in order to yield a definite quantity of output. However, this type of knowledge (of technical recipes) would solve the problem of economic calculation only in the artificial world where either (a) all means of production could be perfectly substituted for each other in definite ratios or (b) each means of production were suitable for one end only.

But in the real world, neither (a) nor (b) is true. Instead, each means of production is more or less suitable for a wide range of ends, and thus each means is substitutable for others but to varying degrees, depending on the task. This fact makes the problem of economic calculation too complex to be solved through engineering knowledge alone. Technology can tell us how many inputs of various kinds will yield a certain output. It cannot tell us which of several possible combinations of inputs is the most "economical" to use when producing a good.

Only money prices can solve the problem of economic calculation. With the use of money, every transaction has one particular good—the universally accepted medium of exchange—on one side, and this gives a common denominator to aid actors in their conduct. A man can look at the infinity of possible ways of taking various combinations of inputs to yield a given output, and he can determine which method is the cheapest. The natural sciences alone cannot provide this type of information.

4. Economic Calculation and the Market

The money prices established in a market are not measurements of value. They are historical facts, recording the ratio at which two items (the money good and some other good or service) exchanged in the past. Even though they are malleable (unlike, say, a chemist's belief in the fixed nature of the charge of an electron), market prices still provide a guide to future action. Without them, all of the subsidiary concepts in accounting (capital and income, profit and loss, spending and saving, cost and yield) would be metaphorical.

Why It Matters

The issue of economic calculation is one of the central themes of the entire book, and Mises breaks up the discussion over several chapters. In this chapter, he focuses on what economic calculation is not—that is, he shows how there are quantitative relationships (in the natural sciences and in our technological know-how) that intersect "economic life," but that these pieces of information alone do not suffice to solve the central problem of economic calculation. Mises briefly states that the solution is money prices, but he doesn't elaborate in this chapter.

Chapter XI: Valuation Without Calculation   *89*

Technical Notes

(1)   Mises singles out the varying specificity of factors
       of production as the key issue in economic calcu-
       lation (pp. 207–08). For example, if a particular
       output good could always be produced by either n
       units of a, or $2n$ units of b, or $3n$ units of c, etc.,
       and moreover this pattern were true of all output
       goods (with possibly different values of n for each
       consumer good), then it would be easy enough to
       value the factors of production. One unit of factor
       a would have the value of 2 units of b and of 3
       units of c, and so forth. And we also know that a
       would have the same value (disregarding the time
       lag needed for production) as $1/n$ units of this par-
       ticular consumer good. Thus, starting with the
       valuation placed on the final consumer goods, the
       completely nonspecific factors of production
       could be valued quite easily.

            On the other hand, if all factors were com-
       pletely specific—meaning that factors a_1 and a_2
       could only be used to produce consumer good A,
       higher-order goods b_1, b_2, and b_3 could only pro-
       duce consumer good B, and so forth—then it
       would be easy enough to value the factors: disre-
       garding the time lag involved, a_1 and a_2 would be
       valued as much as A; b_1, b_2, and b_3 would be valued
       as much as B, and so forth. But things are not so
       simple when the factors can be used in varying

combinations to yield many different types of consumer goods.

(2)   On pages 210–11 Mises alludes to the fact that even the physicists may have to drop the idea of a fixed standard against which to measure absolute quantities. For example, the famous Heisenberg uncertainty principle states that it is impossible to pin down the position and momentum of a subatomic particle beyond a certain degree of accuracy; the very attempt to determine the position of an electron (by firing light at it) will itself change its momentum.

Even so, Mises says that on a macroscopic scale, natural scientists can certainly continue to believe that it makes sense to talk of length, without worrying that meter sticks themselves might change their size unpredictably. Yet this is precisely the problem with economic calculation. Money prices aren't a measurement of subjective value, because money itself is an economic good, subject to changing preferences and diminishing marginal utility as one acquires more units of it.

Study Questions

1. THE GRADATION OF THE MEANS

- How is the gradation of the means similar to that of the ends?

2. THE BARTER-FICTION OF THE ELEMENTARY THEORY OF VALUE AND PRICES

- Why is it necessary to use money prices in order to engage in economic calculation?

- Why does the economist need to first explain the direct barter economy before analyzing the monetary economy?

- What are two principal errors that emerged from the unsatisfactory examination of direct exchange? What were the consequences for the understanding of money and its influence on exchange?

- Is money neutral?

- Does exchange imply that the goods or services involved have equal value?

- Can we measure value?

- What can we say about the valuations of units of a homogeneous supply?

- In what way did the classical doctrines provide a basis for Marxian theories?

3. THE PROBLEM OF ECONOMIC CALCULATION

- Why are money prices necessary for evaluating and comparing the different alternatives and plans that serve at removing uneasiness for the acting man?

- Do economic quantities imply money prices?

4. ECONOMIC CALCULATION AND THE MARKET

Comment: "The distinctive mark of economic calculation is that it is neither based upon nor related to anything which could be characterized as measurement."

- Why do exchange ratios permanently fluctuate?

- Why do economic calculation and the estimation of the expected outcome of future action go hand in hand?

- What is the meaning of economic calculation for human action? How is the concept of economic calculation related to "quantitative sciences of economics"?

CHAPTER XII

THE SPHERE OF ECONOMIC CALCULATION

Chapter Summary

1. THE CHARACTER OF MONETARY ENTRIES

Economic calculation encompasses everything that trades against money. Despite their apparent precision, most of the entries on balance sheets reflect the speculative anticipation of owners regarding future market conditions. Therefore, there is nothing "objective" about them. Even so, economic calculation is as effective as it could be. It cannot give a perfect guide to the future, because the future is inherently uncertain.

2. THE LIMITS OF ECONOMIC CALCULATION

Economic calculation can't account for things that do not exchange for money. Even so, by reducing all other items to a common denominator, economic calculation makes decisions easier for "noneconomic" items. For example, if a financial wizard is choosing between a stressful job at a hedge fund that pays $350,000 per year versus a relaxed life in academia that pays $150,000, economic calculation allows him to boil down the decision to, "If I started in the academic spot, would I prefer to give up the relative peace for an additional $200,000 per year?" The fact that money prices do not eliminate all other judgments is surely not a strike against the conveniences that they do render.

Economic calculation only "works" in the setting of acting men in a market economy, making actual decisions. It makes no sense to discuss the "social value" of a particular policy, as if central planners could perform such computations outside of the haggling on real markets. It also makes no sense to compute the "total income" or wealth of an entire nation. When a firm's capitalization is $1 million, that means (in principle) that if one sold all the assets and paid off all of the liabilities, there would remain $1 million. But this obviously can't be done for the entire wealth of a large nation, let alone for the world as a whole.

3. THE CHANGEABILITY OF PRICES

Prices are in constant flux because their underlying determinants—ultimately the subjective valuations of individuals—are always changing. The popular clamoring for stable prices is due to the lamentable desire to pattern economics after the natural sciences.

4. STABILIZATION

It is understandable why people long for a money with "stable" purchasing power—the terrible experience with government inflation has led to this desire. Nonetheless, the numerous proposals (of various commodity baskets, etc.) for a stable money suffer from insuperable difficulties. These are some of the more important ones:

(1)   Prices are not measured in money; they consist in money. There is no immutable unit of "value" that (even in principle) could be used to define the purchasing power of money.

(2)   The components of a price index change in quality over time; a television set today is not the same thing as a television set in 1950, and thus comparing a dollar today to one in 1950 is arbitrary.

Chapter XII: The Sphere of Economic Calculation 95

(3) The relative importance of the components of a price index can change over time, and there is no nonarbitrary way of gauging this effect. For example, if most people became vegan, then the price of milk and eggs should obviously carry a smaller weight in the commodity basket.

5. THE ROOT OF THE STABILIZATION IDEA

Historically, moneys that originated on the market (such as gold and silver) were adequate for economic calculation, even though they did not possess an eternally fixed "stable" purchasing power. Government inflations changed this and made it imperative for businesspeople to take into account changes in the value of money in their planning and long-term contracts.

Another factor in the popularity of the stabilization idea was the desire for a secure arena outside the uncertainty of the market. People thought the state (with its tremendous might, consuls, and so forth) could provide a shelter for wealth outside the vicissitudes of pleasing the consumers afresh every day.

Why It Matters

In this chapter, Mises lays out the boundaries of economic calculation and explains that, within their sphere, market prices render all the services needed of them. The tools of economic calculation are inappropriate, though, when people extrapolate into areas outside of the actual market. In particular, economic calculation cannot provide a measure of immutable value, because no such thing exists. The efforts to devise a stable money and to provide a flow of guaranteed income are futile.

Technical Notes

(1) Mises writes (p. 223) that the term "price level" is misleading. It suggests that changes originating on the "money side" could affect all prices proportionally, but (as we will see in later chapters) this is impossible. Money isn't neutral, and changes in the supply of money will necessarily cause "real" disturbances, not just nominal ones.

(2) On page 228, Mises critiques the popular claim that war bonds allow the costs of a war to be shunted onto future generations. This is silly because all of the tanks, bombers, etc. consumed by the war effort obviously come out of current production. Of course, a war impoverishes future generations, but only because they inherit a smaller stockpile of capital goods than they otherwise would have.

Chapter XII: The Sphere of Economic Calculation   *97*

Study Questions

1. THE CHARACTER OF MONETARY ENTRIES

- Can we anticipate future prices by looking at prices of the past?

- Why do we have to distinguish between economic calculation as it is practiced by businessmen planning future transactions and those computations of business facts that serve other purposes?

- Can economic calculation expand our information about the future?

2. THE LIMITS OF ECONOMIC CALCULATION

- What are the requirements for economic calculation?

- How can things that don't enter into the items of accountancy and calculation be evaluated and be taken into consideration?

- Why is it nonsensical to compute national income or national wealth?

Comment: "[P]rices are not measured in money; they consist in money."

3. THE CHANGEABILITY OF PRICES

Comment: "The popular notions about money and money prices are not derived from ideas formed in the past. It would be wrong to interpret them as atavistic remnants."

- Why are the ideas of price stability fallacious? Why are they so popular?

4. STABILIZATION

- Why is the conception of stabilization useless in a world of perpetual change?

- Why is it nonsensical to compare baskets of commodities over time in order to define index-number methods? What are the obstacles in regard to technological features of the commodities? Would it be possible to realize it if there weren't these obstacles?

- Why can't other things remain equal if the purchasing power of money changes?

- Does human action imply change? Why?

5. THE ROOT OF THE STABILIZATION IDEA

- What is meant by, "What economic calculation requires is a monetary system whose functioning is not sabotaged by government interference"?

- What are the problems of government bonds?

- How is the interest for government bonds financed?

Chapter XII: The Sphere of Economic Calculation   *99*

> *Comment*: "Financing a war through loans does not shift the burden to the sons and grandsons. It is merely a method of distributing the burden among the citizens."

CHAPTER XIII

MONETARY CALCULATION AS A TOOL OF ACTION

Chapter Summary

1. MONETARY CALCULATION AS A METHOD OF THINKING

Monetary calculation is the guiding principle of action in any society with a division of labor. It transforms the very thought process of anyone considering action that involves the property of others. Potential actions are evaluated on the basis of expected costs and revenues, while past actions are evaluated with the accounting of profit and loss.

Monetary calculation is not simply an outgrowth of action, however. Besides purposeful behavior, monetary calculation requires the institution of private property in the means of production, as well as a universally accepted medium of exchange (i.e., money).

Capitalism was originally a smear term for the system of free enterprise, meant to imply that this system only serves the narrow interests of the capitalists. However, the term is a good one, for the very notion of capital—of summing the market prices of the resources available for a project—is inextricably linked to monetary calculation, which itself can only occur in a capitalist society.

2. ECONOMIC CALCULATION AND THE SCIENCE OF HUMAN ACTION

Praxeology and economics would never have been developed were it not for the historical evolution of economic calculation. Only with money prices and the related concepts of capital, profit, and loss could the early writers have noticed patterns in commercial activity.

Why It Matters

In this very short chapter, Mises stresses the tremendous significance of economic calculation. It is not simply a habit of businesspeople, but rather a distinct mode of thinking. It is necessary for modern civilization, and is the reason for the usefulness of quantitative science. However, Mises underscores the fact that calculation can only work where there is money and where goods of all orders are owned privately.

Technical Notes

(1) Mises claims that monetary calculation is the "guiding star of action" (p. 230). However, action alone does not allow for calculation. In a socialist society or one with only barter, there would still be action—people would still adopt means to achieve ends—but there would be no true economic calculation.

(2) Mises writes that the "measurements of physics and chemistry make sense for practical action only because there is economic calculation" (p. 231). What he means is that the knowledge of the natural sciences alone is not enough to steer the use of scarce resources. Technology may dictate several ways of using resources to yield a desired outcome, but only with money prices can the actor determine which method is "best."

(3) One could, in principle, develop all of the theorems of praxeology without experiencing first-hand a society based on the division of labor and money prices. After all, praxeological results are true a priori. However, in practice, no intellectual would have even thought along these lines had he not grown up in a capitalist society.

Study Questions

1. **MONETARY CALCULATION AS A METHOD OF THINKING**

   Comment: "Monetary calculation is the guiding star of action under the social system of division of labor."

   Comment: "Monetary calculation is entirely inapplicable and useless for any consideration which does not look at things from the point of view of individuals."

   - Can economic calculation expand our information about the future?

2. **ECONOMIC CALCULATION AND THE SCIENCE OF HUMAN ACTION**

   - What is Gresham's law?
   - What is the quantity theory?

Part Four—Catallactics or Economics of the Market Society

CHAPTER XIV

THE SCOPE OF CATALLACTIC PROBLEMS

Chapter Summary

1. THE DELIMITATION OF CATALLACTIC PROBLEMS

The scope of praxeology—the science of human action—is precise: it is the study of goal-seeking, rational behavior. However, the scope of catallactics or specifically "economic" problems is somewhat ambiguous. Economics is mainly concerned with the analysis of how money prices in the real world are formed for all goods and services exchanged on a market. But to do this satisfactorily, economics must be embedded in the broader field of praxeology. In addition, to fully appreciate the functioning of a market economy, the economist must also consider an isolated individual and a socialist community.

The Denial of Economics

Many utopian reformers deny the existence of economic laws. These critics fail to see that scarcity is a fact of the world, and not a byproduct of social institutions or reactionary doctrines.

2. THE METHOD OF IMAGINARY CONSTRUCTIONS

The specific method of praxeology (and economics) is the use of imaginary constructions. For various reasons (to be

105

detailed later), the economist cannot use experiments as the physicist or chemist can to choose among his theories. On the contrary, the economist employs imaginary constructions in a deductive process. He abstracts from the real-world situation the crucial elements in which he is interested, and then either imagines their absence, or tries to pinpoint their exact consequences if present. Precisely because he is imagining a scenario that differs from the actual world, the economist cannot resort to empirical observation to verify or refute his analysis. He must instead examine the validity of each step in the deduction, which leads from the assumptions to the conclusion.

3. THE PURE MARKET ECONOMY

One of the imaginary constructions employed by the economist is the analysis of the pure, unhampered market economy, in which neither the government nor other groups interfere with the voluntary exchange of private property. After working through this analysis, the economist can then proceed to examine the effects of government (or other) interventions into the pure market. Some critics object that this procedure reflects the biases of the orthodox economist, but these critics contradict themselves—they too contrast the (allegedly horrible) operation of a pure market with their own preferred arrangement of government programs. Ironically, when the classical economists extolled the virtues of the "natural" system of a free market, it was because it spontaneously lived up to the ideals of a centrally-planned socialist economy.

The Maximization of Profits

A frequent criticism is that economists erroneously assume that all people act to maximize profit, when in fact there are plenty of people for whom pecuniary gain is less important than other ends. This objection misunderstands praxeology,

Chapter XIV: The Scope and Method of Catallactics   *107*

however. Economics only tells us that, other things equal, a seller seeks the highest price possible, while the buyer seeks the lowest price. Consumers all the time pay more for, say, a steak than for an equally nutritious burger. A worker does not necessarily choose the profession that pays the most, either. These examples are not exceptions to the "rule" of profit maximization, rightly defined, but illustrations of it.

4. THE AUTISTIC ECONOMY

In order to understand interpersonal exchange, economics must analyze autistic exchange, i.e., when an isolated individual "exchanges" less satisfactory for more satisfactory conditions, without interacting with other people.

5. THE STATE OF REST AND THE EVENLY ROTATING ECONOMY

The plain state of rest is not an imaginary construction; it happens whenever there are no transactions, because no buyer wishes to acquire more units of the good or service at the price necessary to induce a seller to surrender more units. The plain state of rest is only transitory; it will be disrupted whenever preferences change and mutually advantageous exchanges once again exist. (And one common way for preferences to change is for producers to create more of the product, lowering their marginal utility for it and making them willing to sell at a price that was unattractive before the new production.)

On the other hand, the final state of rest is indeed an imaginary construction. It refers to the situation in which all of the effects of a particular disturbance have run their course, and the price in question has reached its final price. If a new report causes half of the smokers to quit cold turkey, a plain state of rest in the cigarette market will soon emerge at a much lower price. However, as cigarette manufacturers scale back their

108   *Study Guide to Human Action*

operations and the glut of inventory is reduced to the new level (appropriate for the cut in customers), a new final price will emerge (that may be higher or lower than the previous final price, depending on the specifics).

A final imaginary construction is the evenly rotating economy (ERE), in which all prices have reached their final prices. Since all disturbances have worked their full effects, there is total certainty in the ERE. Production still occurs, as higher-order goods are transformed into lower-order goods; people still go to work and consumers still make purchases. But every day is just like the previous one.

Not only is the ERE imaginary, it is self-contradictory. In a world of perfect certainty, there would be no action. Moreover, in the ERE there would be no need to hold money, and so it is problematic to use the ERE to analyze money prices. Despite these problems, the ERE is indispensable for understanding the difference between interest and profit.

6. THE STATIONARY ECONOMY

A stationary economy is one in which the wealth and income of the individuals remain constant. (An ERE is stationary, but a stationary economy need not be an ERE.) A progressing economy is one in which per capita wealth and income increase, while the opposite happens in a retrogressing economy. In a stationary economy, aggregate profits equal aggregate losses, while profits exceed losses in a progressing economy and vice versa in a retrogressing one.

7. THE INTEGRATION OF CATALLACTIC FUNCTIONS

Economics speaks of the entrepreneur or the laborer, in reference to their economic function. In the real world, the same person can be a capitalist, laborer, and entrepreneur. Economics also uses the terminology for functional distribution, namely,

Chapter XIV: The Scope and Method of Catallactics 109

that the laborer receives wages, the entrepreneur earns profits or losses, the landowner earns rents, and the capitalist earns originary interest.

Why It Matters

In this very important chapter, Mises explains the subject matter of catallactics, which is a subset of the field of praxeology; this is what most people have in mind when they talk of economics. Mises also discusses the specific method that the theoretical economist must use, namely, imaginary constructions. Finally, Mises describes some of the more important imaginary constructions, especially the evenly rotating economy. In essence, Mises lays out in this chapter the boundaries of his subject and describes the tools he will use to analyze it.

Technical Notes

(1) Mises uses the term catallactics to mean "economics in the narrower sense" (p. 235). He defines catallactics as "the analysis of those actions which are conducted on the basis of monetary calculation" (p. 235). Other writers might define catallactics as the study of exchange, which at first blush is broader than Mises's definition (since exchange can occur even if there is no money). However, the two definitions are in practice virtually identical, because Mises writes that a "market in which there is direct exchange only is merely an imaginary construction" (p. 235).

(2) Mises's illustration (p. 245) of the plain state of rest—namely, the daily close of a stock market—is rather unfortunate, for the market closes at a preordained time, and in principle there could be frustrated buyers and sellers who don't exchange simply because of the closing bell. To make matters worse, Mises justifies his choice by pointing out (in footnote 9) that he is disregarding the fluctuations in stock prices over the course of the trading day. A better choice would have been a market in which prices remain fairly stable; then a period in which no sales took place (even though the market is "open") would constitute a plain state of rest.

(3) Of the evenly rotating economy (ERE) Mises writes, "The plain state of rest is disarranged

Chapter XIV: The Scope and Method of Catallactics

again and again, but it is instantly reestablished at the previous level" (p. 248). Recall that in the plain state of rest, no exchanges occur. Yet in the ERE we know that the producers of fifth-order goods sell their wares to the producers of fourth-order goods, and so on. Therefore it must be the case (as Mises claims) that the plain state of rest is constantly (but predictably) upset in the ERE.

Study Questions

1. **THE DELIMITATION OF CATALLACTIC PROBLEMS**

   - How does economics classify actions?

   - What is the field of study of catallactics?

   - What is economics? What should it examine?

   - How does scarcity influence human action?

2. **THE METHOD OF IMAGINARY CONSTRUCTIONS**

   Comment: "An imaginary construction is a conceptual image of a sequence of events logically evolved from the elements of action employed in its formation."

   - Why must we use imaginary constructions in praxeology?

3. **THE PURE MARKET ECONOMY**

   - Is the market obstructed by institutional factors?

   - In what sense can we say that men are always seeking the maximization of profit?

   - In what sense is it absolutely adequate to speak of selfishness when it comes to the question of human action?

- Why do the terms *fair* or *unfair* imply value judgments?

- Does a pure market economy exist? Does the answer affect the conduct of economics?

4. THE AUTISTIC ECONOMY

- Why must economics study the situation of an isolated economic actor?

5. THE STATE OF REST AND THE EVENLY ROTATING ECONOMY

- What is the plain state of rest? Why isn't it an imaginary construction?

- What is the final state of rest?

- What distinguishes the market price from the final price?

- What distinguishes the final state of rest from the evenly rotating economy?

- What is the driving force of the whole market system?

- Why is it not necessary to hold cash in a world without change and certainty?

- Why is the mathematical method to which Mises refers not suited to convey any knowledge?

6. THE STATIONARY ECONOMY

- What distinguishes the stationary economy from the evenly rotating economy?

7. THE INTEGRATION OF CATALLACTIC FUNCTIONS

- What is the role of the promoter in economics?

- What is the role of the entrepreneur in the stationary economy?

- Is the socialist system compatible with the concept of a stationary economy? Is it relevant?

CHAPTER XV

THE MARKET

Chapter Summary

1. THE CHARACTERISTICS OF THE MARKET ECONOMY

The market economy is a social system where individuals specialize in their occupations and the means of production (natural resources, tools, etc.) are privately owned. Although everyone acts to serve his own interests, in a market economy this is achieved by aiming to satisfy the desires of other people.

The market steers individuals into those areas where they can best serve the wants of their fellow men. It does this through voluntary inducements; a person who produces what others desperately desire will make more money than if he spends his day toiling on what he himself thinks is best. Compulsion is the characteristic of the state, which is necessary for a market to function but is itself not part of the (voluntary) relations of the market.

The market is not a place or a thing but rather a process. At any time, the state of the market is summarized by the vast array of prices for all goods and services. These (constantly changing) prices guide individuals as they adjust their conduct to best serve each other in the division of labor. Market prices permit economic calculation, which is the basis of the market economy.

115

2. CAPITAL

Economic calculation rests on the notions of capital and income. The capital associated with a particular enterprise is the estimated sum of money that could be raised if all of the assets were sold and all the liabilities were discharged. Income is the amount of consumption that a particular collection of goods can yield without lowering the capital. If income exceeds consumption, the difference is saving. If consumption exceeds income, the difference is capital consumption.

Capital is a mental concept that makes sense only in a market economy, with actual prices to guide the appraisal of particular items. The term *capital goods* refers to the physical objects that man produces and can be used to augment future production. Although a socialist community would have capital goods, it would only metaphorically have capital, for the latter requires economic calculation to be meaningful.

3. CAPITALISM

History shows that private property goes hand in hand with civilization. Ironically, those who wish economics would become more of an "experimental science" are the ones who ignore this evidence and clamor for interventionism or outright socialism. Although the market economy has never existed in a pure form, the Western civilizations embraced it more and more since the Middle Ages, and because of this, population figures exploded and the standard of living grew fantastically.

The economists must study "pure" capitalism not because they mistakenly think such a system has ever existed, but because economic calculation is only possible in capitalism. Once the benchmark has been analyzed, the chaos of interventionist and socialist approaches can be contrasted with it.

Contrary to popular belief, big business does not necessarily favor laissez-faire, but often seeks government privileges or

Chapter XV: The Market 117

restrictions that at least hamper their smaller competitors more. But to call such interventionism "mature" or "late" capitalism is pure confusion; it is simply that at present, big business does not favor capitalism.

4. THE SOVEREIGNTY OF THE CONSUMERS

Although the entrepreneurs appear to be "in charge" of a market economy, this is a superficial view. In reality, even the head boss must answer to the consumers. The entrepreneur hires laborers, purchases raw materials and equipment, and decides how many factories to build. But if those factories churn out products that no one wants, he will soon lose his "authority."

In a sense, every penny the consumer spends is a vote for that particular product or service. Because the entrepreneurs must compete with each other for scarce factors of production, the consumers ultimately determine which businesses expand and which contract. If an operation shuts down because it can't turn a profit, what that means is that the consumers weren't willing to hand over enough money for the products to allow the entrepreneur to purchase the necessary inputs on the labor and factor markets.

5. COMPETITION

The biological competition in nature, in which the fittest survive and the weak perish, is totally different from the social competition in a market economy. Even though some positions are more coveted than others, all participants benefit from exchanging; there are no "losers" in this competition.

The purpose of social competition is to entrust control of scarce resources to those who are most likely to satisfy the wants of the consumers. Writers often say there is "no competition" in a field dominated by large companies. Yet absent government barriers, newcomers can enter the field provided they have a superior method of serving consumers. The large startup costs and other "barriers" reflect real conditions of scarcity, and to ignore them would be to miss the purpose of competition.

The term "competition" is often used as the antithesis of monopoly. Yet even a monopolist must compete with all other producers for the dollars of the consumers. The true restrictions on competition come from government, not the market.

6. FREEDOM

Freedom and liberty represent the most precious goods to many thinkers in the Western tradition. These terms have meaning only in society; there is no freedom in nature. In interpersonal relations, to be free means to live without being at the mercy of arbitrary decisions of other people.

At first the socialists sneered at the "bourgeois" love of freedom, but it soon became clear that the masses would never support an open restriction of their liberties. Thus the socialists contrasted political and economic freedoms. But if the socialist government controls the press and can assign its critics to work in Siberia, constitutional guarantees of free speech are pointless.

7. INEQUALITY OF WEALTH AND INCOME

People are not born equal, and it is no surprise that the market economy—where incomes are based on how well the consumers are served—yields disparities in wealth and income. However, this inequality is necessary if society is to preserve the freedom of occupation. Without the incentives of higher pay, force must be used to channel workers into areas where they are needed.

Chapter XV: The Market   *119*

8. ENTREPRENEURIAL PROFIT AND LOSS

In the first place, profit and loss are psychic phenomena; an individual profits when he improves his situation according to his subjective value scale. For this very reason, psychic profit and loss can't be measured. However, in a market economy an individual may use the monetary profit or loss as an indication of everyone else's appraisal of his actions. If a farmer can earn more planting tobacco than corn, that doesn't mean he will be happier with the former crop. But it does mean (in a loose sense) that the consumers are indicating a preference for him to plant tobacco.

Even in the evenly rotating economy, where there is no money profit or loss, actors would still achieve psychic profit. In the ERE people still go to work, and consumers still purchase products, all because they hope to achieve greater satisfaction through these actions.

Entrepreneurial profit and loss ultimately stem from the uncertainty of the future. If a man buys factors of production for $1,000 and creates a good that he sells for $10,000 one week later, this is an indication that other entrepreneurs were mistaken in their evaluation of the usefulness of those factors of production. Had others been able to anticipate the future revenues from the good, they too would have entered the factor markets and bid up the "cost" of making the good (and lowered its sale price as more units were created). An entrepreneur earns true profits (over and above what he pays himself as wages for his labor) when he forecasts the future better than others.

9. ENTREPRENEURIAL PROFITS AND LOSSES IN A PROGRESSING ECONOMY

A progressing economy is one in which the per capita quota of capital is increasing. In such an economy, the sum total of entrepreneurial money profits exceeds losses. However, the entrepreneurs do not exhaust the increase in wealth made possible by the additional savings and investment. In order for them to incorporate the additional capital goods into their operations, they must bid up the prices for other factors of production (including labor). This raises the incomes of others in society, which in turn leads them to purchase the increased stock of consumer goods (made possible by the injection of new capital goods). Once the economy has fully adjusted to the new capital goods, the entrepreneurs do not enjoy any lasting increase in income; it has been absorbed by the owners of natural resources and by the workers.

10. PROMOTERS, MANAGERS, TECHNICIANS, AND BUREAUCRATS

Entrepreneurs direct business operations, but they must delegate particular tasks to subordinates. This is made possible through economic calculation: The owner of a giant company can look at the books to determine how much profit (or loss) a particular manager generates in his department. This allows the manager to be given relatively free rein, so long as his branch remains profitable.

In contrast, when an enterprise is not run for profit (such as a police department or a soup kitchen), then the conduct of subordinates must be strictly regulated to ensure that they fulfill the purpose of the enterprise. Otherwise, the fire department could "cut costs" by selling off all of its engines and hoses, and using water bottles to fight fires. This obviously wouldn't serve the consumers, but because taxes fund the agency, they would not go out of business. Hence the government puts in place strict guidelines, i.e., a bureaucracy.

11. THE SELECTIVE PROCESS

The market constantly adjusts to new conditions and "selects" those most capable of handling the scarce resources

Chapter XV: The Market 121

available. In a pure market, there are no privileges and past success is no guarantee of future wealth. If someone comes along who can use factors of production to better serve the consumers, he or she will become wealthier and supplant the incumbent entrepreneurs. Ironically, it is outside of a market economy—such as in medieval times or under interventionist policies—where the rich and powerful had secure positions and didn't need to prove their merit daily.

12. THE INDIVIDUAL AND THE MARKET

Economists often speak of "the market" acting, but the market is simply a collection of individuals. There are no "automatic" market forces, but simply the outcome of each individual's actions. Every producer is also a consumer, and thus "producers' policies" (which simultaneously hurt consumers) are nonsensical.

13. BUSINESS PROPAGANDA

It is true that commercials do not display the highest artistic qualities, but that is because they appeal to the masses. Their purpose is to cultivate desires and transmit information to the bulk of consumers, and (by definition) the majority will not have the refined tastes of the elite. Contrary to popular belief, commercials cannot force people to use inferior products. The sellers of the "truly" better goods can likewise hire ad writers and musicians to compose jingles.

14. THE "VOLKSWIRTSCHAFT"

Volkswirtschaft is a term German statists used to denote the total complex of economic activities directed by the government. It embodies the desire to expand the boundaries of the state in order to acquire resources and achieve self-sufficiency; other countries are viewed as threats and infringements on the growth of the homeland. This mentality is completely alien to the classical liberal who believes in a market economy, where foreign boundaries are irrelevant.

Why It Matters

In this very long and very important chapter, Mises lays out his analysis of the market itself. (The chapter could almost serve as a standalone introduction to free-market economics.) Mises explains what the market really is—a process where millions of individuals interact through voluntary exchanges—and how it gives rise to the quantitative prices that undergird the mental concept of capital and hence of economic calculation. Mises lays out his view of consumer sovereignty, a discussion that explains why he is such a strong supporter of the market economy.

Chapter XV: The Market

Technical Notes

(1) Although Mises himself (p. 271) was aware of the limitations of such terminology, Murray Rothbard was very much opposed to the term "consumer sovereignty," especially as used in the writings of William Hutt. Rothbard stressed that in a market economy, no one has sovereignty over anybody else. The consumers can't force a producer to make something; all they can do is offer him money to do so, just as the employer can only use voluntary payments to persuade workers to join his firm.

(2) In his discussion of monopoly price (p. 278), Mises has in mind a sole producer who faces an inelastic demand curve in the region where the market price would have been, in the absence of monopoly. It seems that Mises thinks that even a monopolist would charge the "nonmonopoly" price if the demand curve was elastic. However, if there are any marginal costs of production, the monopolist will want to restrict production, even if his total revenues drop. Moreover, Rothbard argues that it is nonsensical to contrast the monopoly price with a hypothetical price that would have occurred in the absence of monopoly. If someone invents an entirely new product that no one else had imagined, what is the "nonmonopoly" price and output to which the innovator's price and output should be compared?

(3) Mises argues that capital accumulation necessarily leads to an excess of money profits over losses (pp. 292–95). Strictly speaking this needn't be true: if everyone perfectly anticipated a steady accumulation in capital per capita over a ten-year period, prices would adjust so that no profits were earned during the decade. It appears that Mises has in mind a scenario where the injection of new savings catches most people by surprise. (More generally, Mises doesn't entertain the notion of a certain future where things still change; i.e., he reserves a zero-profit world for the ERE.)

Chapter XV: The Market 125

Study Questions

1. **THE CHARACTERISTICS OF THE MARKET ECONOMY**

   - What are the main characteristics of the market economy?

   - What is meant by "the market is a process"?

   Comment: "There is no mixture of the two systems possible . . . there is no such thing as a mixed economy, a system that would be in part capitalistic and in part socialist."

2. **CAPITAL**

   - What are the definitions of capital, capital consumption, and saving?

   - Why is it impossible to separate the concept of capital from the context of monetary calculation?

   - What is the notion of real capital? Why is it nonsensical?

3. **CAPITALISM**

   Comment: "The market economy is a man-made mode of acting under the division of labor. But this does not imply that it is something accidental or artificial and could be replaced by another mode."

Comment: "Entrepreneurs grown old and tired and the decadent heirs of people who succeeded in the past dislike the agile parvenus who challenge their wealth and their eminent social position."

4. THE SOVEREIGNTY OF THE CONSUMERS

- Who really determines what is produced?

- What is the role of the entrepreneur?

Comment: "The entrepreneurs, capitalists, and farmers have their hands tied; they are bound to comply in their operations with the orders of the buying public."

- What is the difference between a political democracy and a free market with regard to the power of votes?

- Why is it absolutely fallacious to compare big companies with kingdoms? What is the main difference between a company and a political sovereign?

5. COMPETITION

- What is the difference between biological competition and social competition?

- What is meant by catallactic competition? To which field is it restricted? Why is it a social phenomenon?

Chapter XV: The Market 127

- What are the two connotations of monopoly? What is the significance of each for the market?

- Why can we safely neglect the existence of monopolies if there are no monopoly prices that emerge?

- What are monopoly prices, in Mises's view?

6. FREEDOM

- Are freedom and liberty to be found in nature?

Comment: "A man is free as far as he can live and get on without being at the mercy of arbitrary decisions on the part of other people."

- How are the terms *liberty* and *freedom* related to the state and the market economy?

- Why were the socialist doctrines—which reversed the original meaning of the terms *liberty* and *freedom*—able to triumph, according to Mises?

- What is the confusion behind the slogan, "Planning for Freedom"?

7. INEQUALITY OF WEALTH AND INCOME

- Is it necessary to guarantee equality of income in order to obtain freedom?

- When is compulsion justified, according to Mises?

8. ENTREPRENEURIAL PROFIT AND LOSS

- Why does Mises say profit and loss are in their original sense psychic phenomena? Can they be measured? Why or why not?

- What role do the complementary factors of production and the final product play for entrepreneurial profit?

- What are the main reasons for entrepreneurial loss?

- What information do the prices of the factors of production provide for us?

- What is the ultimate source from which entrepreneurial profits and losses are derived?

9. ENTREPRENEURIAL PROFITS AND LOSSES IN A PROGRESSING ECONOMY

- What is the definition of a progressing economy?

- Why can't the surplus of the total sum of entrepreneurial profits exhaust the total increase in wealth by economic progress?

- Who benefits from an increase of productivity?

- Do we have to draw a sharp line between short-run and long-run effects?

- How can a surplus of the total sum of all entrepreneurial profits over all entrepreneurial losses come into existence?

Chapter XV: The Market 129

- Who contributes to economic progress?

- Is there still entrepreneurial activity in a retro-gressing economy? Why?

- Why is the socialist concept of "unearned income" fallacious?

- What is Mises's critique of the underconsumption doctrine?

10. **PROMOTERS, MANAGERS, TECHNICIANS, AND BUREAUCRATS**

- What distinguishes the entrepreneur from the manager?

Comment: "Economic calculation as practiced in the market economy . . . makes it possible to relieve the entrepreneur of involvement in too much detail."

- What is the significance of double-entry book-keeping?

- What is the difference between bureaucratic management and profit management?

11. **THE SELECTIVE PROCESS**

Comment: "The market makes people rich or poor, determines who shall run the big plants and who shall scrub the floors, fixes how many people shall work in the copper mines and how many in the symphony orchestras."

- Why is ownership a liability?

- Why is it not right to pretend that "penniless" people are not able to climb the ladder of wealth and entrepreneurial position? What is the role of institutions?

- Why doesn't a degree in business administration imply a career as an entrepreneur?

12. THE INDIVIDUAL AND THE MARKET

- What is meant by the statement, "The market is a social body"? Why are interventionist policies not necessary to "humanize" the market?

- What does Mises think of the distinction made between a "producers' policy" versus a "consumers' policy"? What is the psychological root of the producers' policy, as practiced by governments in the 20th century?

- What is the lesson of the story of the man asking an innkeeper for ten dollars?

13. BUSINESS PROPAGANDA

- What is the definition of advertising according to Mises?

- How can advertising influence the choice of consumers? Is it relevant for praxeology?

- Why are business and political propaganda essentially different things?

- What is meant by, "Freedom is indivisible"?

Chapter XV: The Market 131

- Do advertising costs constitute part of production costs?

14. THE "VOLKSWIRTSCHAFT"

- What is the definition of the "Volkswirtschaft"?

- What is meant by "Gemeinnutz geht vor Eigennutz"?

- What is the meaning of "Lebensraum"?

- Is "Volkswirtschaft" compatible with the free market?

- Under which conditions is "Volkswirtschaft" realized?

CHAPTER XVI

PRICES

Chapter Summary

1. THE PRICING PROCESS

When two individuals trade goods as an isolated event, catallactics can only say that the exchange ratio in this act of barter will ensure that each trader gains something more valuable than what he gives up. Beyond that truism, the exchange ratio (barter "price") could be anywhere in a wide range. However, in an organized market with many buyers and sellers of the same item, the modern theory of price formation explains that the price must fall within narrow limits (as explained in the "Technical Notes" below).

The modern, subjectivist theory of prices does not assume that people have "perfect knowledge" of the market. On the contrary, catallactics can explain the formation of actual prices in the real world. Indeed, those mainstream economists who study static "equilibrium" outcomes ignore the crucial process in which speculative entrepreneurs drive the market toward equilibrium. By spotting disequilibrium (but real-world) prices and acting to seize the profit opportunities that they entail, it is the entrepreneurs who move the whole system toward the equilibrium state that the mathematical economists take for granted

133

as the starting point of analysis. By buying "underpriced" goods or factors of production, and selling "overpriced" ones, the entrepreneurs push up the former and push down the latter prices, earning profits and equilibrating the economy.

2. VALUATION AND APPRAISEMENT

All prices are ultimately formed because of the subjective valuation of the consumers. We must always remember that the price that results from an act of exchange is not determined by an equality of values (e.g., "one car equals 30,000 dollars") but rather a difference in valuation (e.g., the seller values the 30,000 dollars more than the car, while the buyer values the car more than his 30,000 dollars).

Appraisement is different; it is an objective assessment of how much money an item will fetch in the market. Though the subjective valuations of consumers ultimately explain these prices, the appraiser himself needn't consider his personal opinion of the utility of the object being evaluated. Even so, in a modern economy, even the consumer must act as an appraiser. This is because to gauge the true cost of a purchase, the consumer must consider what other goods and services could be acquired with the money instead. To answer this question, the consumer must be familiar with the purchasing power of money, i.e., with the typical prices of goods and services that he might desire instead.

3. THE PRICES OF THE GOODS OF HIGHER ORDERS

The economist explains the prices of higher-order goods (i.e., factors of production) in the same way that he explains the prices of consumer goods, i.e., by first explaining what motivates purchases and then by imagining what conditions would cause the market to cease. When it comes to consumers, they purchase products so long as the units they acquire are valued

Chapter XVI: Prices   *135*

more highly than the money they trade away. With entrepreneurs in the markets for factors of production, the same is true. However, unlike consumers, they do not value their purchases for the direct utility they provide. On the contrary, the entrepreneurs evaluate factors of production based on their appraisal of the products that these factors can create. Thus, subjective consumer valuations determine the prices of the first-order goods, and then appraising entrepreneurs forecast these prices in order to guide their buying decisions, which lead to the formation of the prices of 2nd-, 3rd-, and higher-order goods.

4. COST ACCOUNTING

For the entrepreneur, costs are the money required to purchase the factors of production. Naturally, the entrepreneur seeks out factors of production with prices low enough to allow him to create and sell a product, earning enough revenue to cover his explicit costs. Determining the optimal quantity of factors to purchase is a complicated task because (for technological reasons) proportional increases in inputs do not always yield proportional increases in yield.

Although there are strict rules of accountancy (both for shareholders and tax purposes), we must remember that the entrepreneur is always guided by his forecasts of likely future prices. At any time, there is no "fact of the matter" of the capital value of a given inventory; what matters is not how much the firm paid for the inputs, but rather what the firm is likely to get when it sells the inventory in the future (and what the relevant interest rate will be in the interim).

5. LOGICAL CATALLACTICS VERSUS MATHEMATICAL CATALLACTICS

The mathematical economists deride the "literary" approach, believing that only empirical measurement is scientific. But there are no constants in human action, as there are in the natural sciences (charge of an electron, speed of light in a vacuum, etc.). The statistical analysis of prices is merely a study of economic history, as past prices have no necessary relation to future ones. The mathematical study of prices also proceeds as if there is no monetary good or market process, and hence entirely misconstrues the way prices are formed in the real world. Finally, the attempt to model the differential equations of classical mechanics is faulty. The physicist can describe the motion of a ball in a vacuum at any point in time, but he doesn't know "why" the ball moves. In contrast, the praxeologist knows why men exchange in a market, but he can't predict beforehand the actual market price at any moment (because, in reality, any such price will be a "disequilibrium" one, while the equations refer to hypothetical equilibrium prices).

6. MONOPOLY PRICES

The sovereignty of the consumer is violated only very rarely on a free market, namely, when the sole seller (or a group of all sellers acting in concert) finds it profitable to restrict output and raise the price above what the competitive price would have been. The monopolist will only be able to do this when the demand curve is inelastic at the competitive price (meaning the seller will receive more total revenues by raising the price and selling fewer units), and when the seller can't discriminate among the buyers. (If the monopolist could segment the market, charging different prices for each group, then he wouldn't need to restrict output in order to maximize profit.)

It is important to realize that being a "monopolist" per se is insignificant. If we define the product or service narrowly enough, every producer is a monopolist. (Only one person can sell Mary Rosen's litigation services.) For Mises, the seller violates consumer sovereignty only when he restricts output below what the consumers desire, i.e., below the competitive level.

Chapter XVI: Prices

7. GOOD WILL

Because people are endowed with different information and areas of expertise, buyers often must rely on the integrity of the seller. As a particular producer gains trust over time, this "good will" gives him an advantage over competitors who lack it. Many paternalist reformers wish to substitute government certification for the market's response to "asymmetric information," but if the government appointees are themselves fallible (or corrupt), this is no solution. Though inefficient when compared to a world where people are omniscient, the market outcome of brand-name recognition and trust overcomes the problem of asymmetric information.

8. MONOPOLY OF DEMAND

If there is a single buyer, or if all of the buyers act in concert, they can restrict demand in order to lower the price. However, they will necessarily buy (and hence enjoy) fewer units of the good compared to the status quo. Thus the "monopolistic" buyer cannot earn a specific gain the way a monopolistic seller can.

9. CONSUMPTION AS AFFECTED BY MONOPOLY PRICES

Generally speaking, the happiness of consumers is impaired by monopoly prices. The one exception is a situation where a product would not be produced at all, were it not for monopoly prices in one of its essential inputs. (This is the justification for granting monopolies—in the form of patents or copyrights—to the creators of "intellectual property.")

Most discussions of monopoly are confused. In a free market, only a few minerals and local network goods (phone lines, electricity) would have monopoly prices. In reality, it is government privileges that establish cartels and monopolies.

10. PRICE DISCRIMINATION ON THE PART OF THE SELLER

Generally, economists discuss market prices as if there is a single price prevailing for "the same" good or service. However, it is sometimes possible for a seller to charge different prices based on a particular customer's willingness to pay. This can only happen if it is difficult for the buyers to resell the good among themselves, and it will only happen if the seller will thereby gain more profit than if he had charged a uniform price. The textbook example of price discrimination is a country doctor who charges more from his wealthy clients than from his poor ones.

Specific clients may be hurt by price discrimination, but it is possible that a certain good will only be provided if price discrimination occurs.

11. PRICE DISCRIMINATION ON THE PART OF THE BUYER

Although monopolistic buyers cannot achieve monopoly prices (and monopoly gains), they can conceivably benefit from price discrimination, i.e., from paying different prices to different sellers. This situation would not persist on a free market, however, because it relies on the crass ignorance of the sellers.

12. THE CONNEXITY OF PRICES

The prices of certain goods have a special connection; a sale on peanut butter may affect the price of jelly. But even more generally, the prices of all goods are related because they all compete for the money of buyers. And since labor is required for every good, they are all interrelated on both the consumption and production side. It is impossible to analyze a particular price in isolation.

Chapter XVI: Prices

13. PRICES AND INCOME

The market process does not engage in distinct activities of price determination and income determination (or production versus "distribution"). The market process entails the definite exchange ratios in actual, specific transactions. It is only a subjective attitude that views a capital good (or even land or labor) as a source of income. Only the successful, acting individual can maintain capital equipment or his body in order to continually sell goods or services in the future to reap this anticipated flow of "income."

14. PRICES AND PRODUCTION

The market process directs the factors of production into those lines that best satisfy the desires of the consumers. In a free market, there cannot be long-run unemployment of labor, as labor is the ultimate nonspecific factor. However, there can be sustained unemployment of specific land or even capital goods—"idle capacity." So long as this outcome occurs on a free market, it represents the most efficient use of resources, given the mistakes of the past. For the government to pass legislation to spur employment of these factors (hence ignoring reality) only makes the consumers poorer.

15. THE CHIMERA OF NONMARKET PRICES

It is nonsense to speak of prices besides those formed in the actual market. There are always segments of the population who would benefit from higher (or lower) prices for a particular good or service, but their desire for a different price in no way impugns the actual price. Because market prices take into account all relevant facts, those attempting to alter prices would necessarily be ignoring these real considerations. For example, if the government requires an equal price for all types of running shoes, this will not eliminate the fact that the consumers really do "arbitrarily" value some brands more than others.

Why It Matters

In yet another long and important chapter, Mises lays out the nature of prices and (briefly) sketches how they are actually formed.

(A more elaborate treatment of the formation of specific prices is in Rothbard's *Man, Economy, and State*.)

Mises is very clear on the complicated but crucial relationship between subjective consumer valuations and objective prices of the factors of production. The material in this chapter is necessary to fully understand Mises's critique of socialism.

Technical Notes

(1) In the beginning of the chapter (p. 324), Mises somewhat obliquely refers to the limits set on a market price with many buyers and sellers. He has in mind a large market with individuals initially having different amounts of the good in question, and then some individuals trade with each other at a uniform price, while others refrain from trade. If we assume that a certain number of units are bought and sold at a common price—and that every buyer and seller has transacted exactly the number of units desired—then it must be the case that the price is low enough to induce the "marginal buyer" to purchase the last unit being traded and to simultaneously prevent the "marginal offerer" from being willing to sell an additional unit, and high enough to induce the "marginal seller" to sell the last unit traded and also high enough to prevent the "marginal potential buyer" from wanting to purchase an additional unit.

(For this argument to work, we must assume that every trader knows what the common price is. That's why Rothbard actually titles this section "Determination of Price: Equilibrium Price" in *Man, Economy, and State*.)

(2) Mises says,

> It is permissible to declare that, due allowance being made for time preference,

the value attached to a product is equal to
the value of the total complex of complementary factors of production. (p. 332)

His purpose with this concession is to distinguish
such a claim from the truly erroneous approach of
many economists in which they declare that the
subjective value of the final consumer good is
equal to the sum of the subjective valuations of
the factors that contribute to its production.
However, even Mises's concession goes too far,
because in practice no single individual knows all
of the factors (and what quantity of each) required
for something as simple as a pencil. Therefore,
even though it is not nonsense to say that the factors needed to make a pencil are (in their totality)
valued the same as a (future) pencil, it is a rather
empty statement, since no one is in a position to
make such a "permissible" valuation.

(3) Murray Rothbard rejected the distinction
between a monopoly price and a so-called "competitive price." Rothbard argued that only government privileges could establish monopoly
prices, and that all the economist had were real-
world free-market levels of output. Every producer "restricts" output if so doing yields more
profit, and since there is no such thing as a hypothetical "competitive" level to use as a benchmark,
there are no grounds for criticizing some of these
producers.

Chapter XVI: Prices

Study Questions

1. THE PRICING PROCESS

- What does every exchange imply with regard to the value attached by each party?

- Why is the concept of perfect information useless for the explanation of prices?

- How is the inequality of people important for understanding of the market process?

- Who are the driving forces of the market process? How do they interact?

- Do entrepreneurs take into account final or equilibrium prices?

Comment: "[C]atallactics shows that entrepreneurial activities tend toward an abolition of price differences not caused by the costs of transportation and trade barriers."

2. VALUATION AND APPRAISEMENT

- What is the ultimate source of the determination of prices?

- What distinguishes appraisement from valuation?

- Is the notion of a "fair price" scientific?

3. THE PRICES OF THE GOODS OF HIGHER ORDERS

- In what way are the prices of the goods of the higher order determined by the goods of the first or lower order?

- Does the pricing process of higher-order goods involve a connection of subjective values?

- Which method do we owe to Gossen, Menger, and Böhm-Bawerk?

- Why would it be absurd to speak of a sum of valuations or values?

- Why don't the prices of the past influence future prices?

- What is the pricing process if the production of a product requires two or more absolutely specific factors? What would be the pricing process if all factors of production were specific?

4. COST ACCOUNTING

- What is meant by the law of increasing returns or decreasing costs?

- What would happen if all of the imperfectly divisible factors were utilized at less than full capacity? What would be the result of an expansion of production? What would happen when full utilization of the capacity of one of the imperfectly divisible factors was attained?

Chapter XVI: Prices

- How do transportation costs relate to prices of the factors of production?

- Why aren't fixed costs determined merely by technological reasoning?

5. LOGICAL CATALLACTICS VERSUS MATHEMATICAL CATALLACTICS

- What are the main currents of thought in the field of mathematical economics?

- Why does the statistical approach imply the presentation of historical facts? Why does this make it inappropriate for economics?

- In what way can a datum of experience or a statistical fact add to the understanding of the determination of prices?

- What are the objectives of the investigations of the relations of prices and costs applied by mathematical economists? What is the role of money within the analysis?

- Why are calculations on the basis of units of utility nonsensical?

- What are two fundamental principles of the theory of value?

6. MONOPLY PRICES

- What are the special conditions required for the emergence of monopoly prices? Give a short overview.

- Why isn't a monopoly the only prerequisite for the emergence of monopoly prices?

- Why is it fallacious to assume a third category of prices? What are the roots of this problem?

- According to Mises, how is the control of supply misinterpreted?

- Why does entrepreneurial profit have nothing to do with monopoly?

- What is a cartel? Is it harmful to an economy?

- Is the number of competitors important for competition?

- What are optimum monopoly prices?

- What is meant by an incomplete monopoly? What are the consequences?

- In what way is free entry into the branch of production decisive for the preservation of cartels? What is the importance of this fact for analysis of monopolies?

- What is the role of licenses with regard to the formation of monopoly prices?

- What is meant by a failure monopoly?

- Why do labor unions not aim at monopoly prices?

- What can mathematics teach us about the demand curve of monopolies?

7. GOOD WILL

- What is the meaning of good will? What are some of Mises's examples?

8. MONOPOLY OF DEMAND

- How does a monopoly of demand differ from a "competition" of demand?

- How can an apparent monopoly of demand turn out to be a monopoly of supply?

9. CONSUMPTION AS AFFECTED BY MONOPOLY PRICES

- What are the different reactions possible *vis-à-vis* monopoly prices? Give a short overview.

- In which case would the reactions of the consumers create a situation where the price under monopoly equaled the competitive price?

- What would be the situation if all consumers spent less for a product under a monopoly price than under the competitive price?

- What is the argument in favor of patent and copyright legislation?

- How does government interventionism influence the formation of cartels and monopolies?

10. PRICE DISCRIMINATION ON THE PART OF THE SELLER

- What conditions must be met in order to make price discrimination advantageous?

- How can price discrimination render the satisfaction of a need possible that would have remained unsatisfied in its absence?

11. PRICE DISCRIMINATION ON THE PART OF THE BUYER

- Can price discrimination by the buyer occur without government intervention?

12. THE CONNEXITY OF PRICES

- Why does the fact that labor is nonspecific bring about the general connexity of all human activities?

13. PRICES AND INCOME

- Why is income a category of action? What does it mean?

- Can there be a "safe" income?

- Can market incomes accurately be viewed as a distribution?

14. PRICES AND PRODUCTION

- What do prices determine for the production process?

Chapter XVI: Prices

- Why is it nonsense to lament the fact of unused capacity?

- What is malinvestment?

15. THE CHIMERA OF NONMARKET PRICES

- Is there such a thing as "real costs"?

- Why is the idea of cost prices fallacious?

CHAPTER XVII

INDIRECT EXCHANGE

Chapter Summary

1. MEDIA OF EXCHANGE AND MONEY

In direct exchange, each party intends to use the object being acquired for consumption or production. In contrast, during indirect exchange, at least one of the parties to the transaction does not intend to personally use the item being acquired. He plans to trade it away in the future for some other item. This is why the object is a *medium* of exchange: just as air is a medium through which sound waves are transmitted, so too can an economic good serve as the medium through which a more ultimate exchange is effected.

When one particular good is used as a medium of exchange by most members of the community—when it serves as the "commonly used" medium of exchange—then it is *money*. All moneys are media of exchange, but not all media of exchange attain the status of money.

2. OBSERVATIONS ON SOME WIDESPREAD ERRORS

The "equation of exchange" is a typical yet obsolete approach to the analysis of money. It asserts that MV=PQ; that

151

is, the aggregate stock of money (M) times the "velocity of circulation" of money (V) must equal the "price level" (P) times the quantity of real output (Q). From this identity, economists derived the faulty notion of the "neutrality of money," which asserted that a given increase in the stock of money could proportionally raise all prices.

Yet this is reasoning in a circle. The argument starts out with the assumption that "level of prices" and "total output" are meaningful concepts. This is not how economists approach other issues in economic theory. When explaining the price of apples, the economist looks at the individual actor and his marginal utility for apples; he doesn't consider the class of all apples. The same approach works with explaining the "price" (i.e., purchasing power) of money.

There is one important difference between the economist's task in explaining the purchasing power of money, versus explaining the price of other goods such as apples or televisions. For these other goods, the economist takes the actor's valuation of them as a given fact, which can be handled by the psychologists and physiologists. But it is the economist's job to explain why a man should value a specific unit of money in the first place, and to trace out the implications of that valuation.

3. DEMAND FOR MONEY AND SUPPLY OF MONEY

Some goods are more marketable (or "liquid") than others. This means that a seller of such goods would not have to search very long to find a buyer willing to pay the highest likely price that anyone would offer for the good. In contrast, if the seller of an unmarketable (or illiquid) good has to dispose of it quickly, he will have to accept a much lower price than what he would be able to obtain if he had more time to find a suitable buyer.

It is the difference in marketability of various goods that gives rise to media of exchange. For example, if a farmer wishes

Chapter XVII: Indirect Exchange   *153*

to trade away a pig in exchange for sweaters, but cannot find someone who wants to trade away sweaters for a pig, then the farmer can still improve his situation by trading away the pig for something that is more marketable, such as tobacco. Not only is he more likely to find someone who wants to trade away sweaters for tobacco, but it is much easier to store and transport the tobacco than the live pig.

Money provides its unique services when it resides in someone's cash balance. There is no such thing as money "in circulation"; at any moment, every unit of money belongs to someone's cash balance. For this reason, there is nothing to distinguish the "hoarder's" cash balance from that of a "normal" person, except for their relative size.

The Epistemological Import of Carl Menger's Theory of the Origin of Money

The different degree of marketability among goods forms the basis of Carl Menger's theory of the spontaneous origin of money. We do not have to posit a wise king who conceived of the benefits of indirect exchange, and instructed his subjects accordingly. We need only assume that people in direct exchange began behaving as our hypothetical farmer above. As people increased their demand for marketable goods (for use as media of exchange), this would increase their marketability even more so. The process would snowball until only a few goods —such as gold and silver—served as the media of exchange to which everyone turned. At that point, money emerged, though no one had planned the outcome.

4. THE DETERMINATION OF THE PURCHASING POWER OF MONEY

The "price" of money is its exchange value in the market place; it is the vast array of goods and services at any moment that others are willing to offer for a unit of the money. For a commodity money such as gold, its market value depends on its industrial demand as well as its monetary demand; people offer valuable items for gold because they wish to use it in production or consumption, but also because they wish to hold it as a medium of exchange. (The special case of fiat money, which has no industrial or consumption use, will be handled in section 9.)

Economists were reluctant to use the standard marginal-utility approach to the price of money because of an apparent paradox. The monetary component of the demand for money is clearly due to its exchange value; people are willing to labor for an hour in exchange for a certain quantity of gold, because they believe that they can obtain food, shelter, and other items later on in exchange for the gold. But this seems to argue in a circle: it says that the money has marginal utility because it possesses exchange value, while it explains the exchange value of money by reference to its marginal utility!

Mises showed the way out of this impasse. To explain the purchasing power of money right now, we rely on people's expectations about the *future* purchasing power of money. And these expectations in turn come about from the experience of money's purchasing power in the recent past. In short, the purchasing power of money *today* is grounded on the expectations of its purchasing power *tomorrow*, where this forecast is based on its purchasing power *yesterday*. The economist is thus not saying, "We explain the exchange value of money by reference to the exchange value of money," but rather, "We explain today's exchange value of money by reference to yesterday's exchange value of money."

Mises also deals with the next objection, which is that the new argument leads to an infinite regress. This too is a faulty claim, because the process stops when the exchange value for the money is traced back to the days of direct exchange. At that point, the commodity was demanded solely for its direct use in

Chapter XVII: Indirect Exchange

production or consumption, when there is no question of the applicability of marginal-utility theory.

Other things equal, an increase in the supply of money will diminish its exchange value, i.e., the money prices of all other goods and services will rise. However, it is a crass error to assume that an injection of new money will lead to proportional increases in all money prices. On the contrary, certain individuals will spend the new money more quickly than others, causing the prices of only certain goods to rise while other prices lag behind. During the adjustment period, wealth will be redistributed into the hands of those who spend the new money early in the process.

5. The Problem of Hume and Mill and the Driving Force of Money

It is understandable that in response to the massive inflations in interwar Germany and other countries, people long for a money with stable purchasing power. Yet this is an impossible goal, as we have seen that changes in the supply of and demand for money affect prices unevenly. It is also nonsense to hope for a neutral money, which has no driving force of its own. Such a good would not be a "perfect" money; it would not be money at all.

6. Cash-Induced and Goods-Induced Changes in Purchasing Power

Changes in the exchange ratio between money and the various goods and services can arise either from the side of money or from the "real" side. Typically, changes in the purchasing power of money across most items can only occur from the money side.

Changes originating from the money side cannot make the community richer; they can only redistribute wealth, and this is true even if we disregard the matter of deferred payments. On the other hand, if the purchasing power of money increases because of a general increase in the supply of real goods and services, then some can be richer without a corresponding impoverishment of anyone else.

Any quantity of money can provide its full services to the community, in its role as medium of exchange. Expanding the money supply only enriches the community to the extent that a larger quantity is available for nonmonetary purposes.

Inflation and Deflation; Inflationism and Deflationism

The terms *inflation* and *deflation* used to signify cash-induced changes in the purchasing power of money. Yet the terms are now used in a narrower sense, to denote merely the rise or fall in the so-called "level of prices." This new usage is unfortunate because it prevents the public from laying the blame on the true cause of price increases, i.e., increases in the supply of money.

7. MONETARY CALCULATION AND CHANGES IN PURCHASING POWER

For the purposes of economic calculation, the businessman must decide upon a money in which to reckon. If the prevailing money is deemed too unstable, he may switch to another, but then he must deal with the unavoidable changes in purchasing power for this money. Under a gold standard, businessmen historically did not bother using index numbers or other devices to adjust their books for changes in the purchasing power of gold.

8. THE ANTICIPATION OF EXPECTED CHANGES IN PURCHASING POWER

If people generally expect the purchasing power of money to change, they will adjust their cash holdings accordingly and

Chapter XVII: Indirect Exchange   157

speed up the process. For example, if prices in general are expected to rise, then people will lower their cash holdings and seek to acquire goods while they are relatively cheap. But this very reaction will itself push up prices. If the public ever becomes convinced that the rise in prices will continue to accelerate, they will completely abandon the currency in a "flight to real values," causing the "crackup boom."

9. The Specific Value of Money

A *commodity money* is one that serves nonmonetary purposes; an example is gold. *Credit money* evolved out of the use of money substitutes, when the heretofore-prompt redemption of claims to money became suspect. At that point, the claims that previously circulated at par with the actual money traded at a discount, due to the uncertainty of the claim. However, they were still partially valued in their role as a medium of exchange. If a credit money loses its character as a claim against money proper, it can still conceivably circulate as a *fiat money*, which is valued solely for its use as a medium of exchange.

Holding cash balances requires a definite sacrifice, as the owner of a specific quantity of money must forego the goods for which it could immediately be traded, and the interest it could earn if lent. This consideration demonstrates that money provides services merely by resting "idle" in one's cash balance.

10. The Import of the Money Relation

In times of economic distress, people often blame a "lack of money." Yet widespread dislocations in production are the outcome of previous monetary disturbances (to be explained in chapter XX). To end a crisis and restore employment, real factors of production need to be rearranged to those lines where they will best serve the desires of consumers, and interference with the supply of money (in an attempt to thwart this readjustment) will only prolong the crisis.

11. The Money-Substitutes

If there is a claim to a definite amount of money, payable and redeemable on demand, such that no one doubts the solvency of the debtor, then this claim performs all the services of money and becomes a *money substitute*. Typical examples are banknotes and bank demand deposits subject to check.

If the debtor, such as a bank, has kept a reserve of money proper to "back up" the money substitutes that it has issued, the claims are called *money certificates*. However, if the debtor has issued more money substitutes than it can redeem with money proper, then the "unbacked" portion of the claims become *fiduciary media*.

12. The Limitation on the Issuance of Fiduciary Media

A bank or government naturally has the incentive to issue fiduciary media, but there are limits. If the issuance proceeds so rapidly that the public becomes suspicious, they will turn in the claims and demand redemption in actual money. In a competitive market, the limits are even narrower. A single bank will only enjoy a subset of the population as its clients; anyone else who receives its banknotes will not add them to cash balances. Therefore a bank that unilaterally inflated its issuance of fiduciary media would quickly find these excess notes returning for redemption.

Observations on the Discussions Concerning Free Banking

All of the alleged horrors that would occur under unregulated banking are in fact due to government privileges that relieve certain banks from their contractual obligations. Without

Chapter XVII: Indirect Exchange 159

government protection (in the form of "bank holidays," etc.), irresponsible banks would be subject to runs and would go bankrupt. The bogey of a cartel of private banks, expanding in unison, is nonsense; the banks with better reputations would not join the others. Moreover, the entire aim of the government in banking has been to cartelize the industry and promote credit expansion (in order to lower interest rates) that would not occur in a free market.

13. THE SIZE AND COMPOSITION OF CASH HOLDINGS

People decide on the proper size of cash holdings on the basis of subjective marginal utility. Generally speaking, what matters to a person is not the absolute quantity of money held, but its purchasing power. Although people may always desire more *wealth* (measured in money), it is not true that they always desire additional cash balances. It is entirely possible for someone to be holding "too much" cash, and he will take steps to reduce the holding.

14. BALANCES OF PAYMENTS

The *balance of payments* is the record of the money equivalent of the incomings and outgoings of an individual or group during a specific period of time. The credit side and debit side are necessarily equal; the balance of payments is always in balance.

The modern view that a net outflow of money reflects a "negative" balance of trade is due to Mercantilist prejudices. A trade "deficit" is not an unforeseen calamity that strikes a nation, but rather the cumulative outcome of deliberate transactions undertaken by each individual within the nation. No one worries that the residents of New York might foolishly spend all of their money on wares from the other states. The situation is more complicated when other countries and foreign currencies are involved, but the principle is the same.

160   *Study Guide to Human Action*

15. INTERLOCAL EXCHANGE RATES

Arbitrage opportunities keep exchange rates between moneys within narrow limits. Just as the prices for other commodities in different locations can only differ by the shipping costs involved—for if the difference were greater, then merchants would buy at the cheap location and sell in the dear location—so too can the purchasing power of different moneys differ only by a small margin. One important difference between money and other commodities is that there is a predictable pattern in the prices of the latter; they are lowest near their areas of production and rise with shipping costs as one moves farther away.

When a government inflates the currency, domestic prices rise unevenly. It may happen that the currency falls on the foreign-exchange market early in the process. This leads to the silly charge that speculators are to blame for the price increases, since they "attacked" the domestic currency.

16. INTEREST RATES AND THE MONEY RELATION

Credit transactions carried out in the same currency tend to yield the same interest rates for comparable credit risks. When money is borrowed in one currency and lent in another, the investor must take into account not only the different interest rates involved but also the possible change in exchange rates during the life of the loans.

17. SECONDARY MEDIA OF EXCHANGE

The fact that one or more media of exchange have risen to the status of money does not eliminate the differences in marketability among the remaining goods. Those items that are still quite marketable—though not as much as the money good—will enjoy a demand for both their "original" use but also because of their marketability; in this respect they can be

Chapter XVII: Indirect Exchange   161

considered as secondary media of exchange. Those holding these secondary media can carry smaller cash balances accordingly. Typical examples include government and high-grade corporate bonds.

18. THE INFLATIONIST VIEW OF HISTORY

The general public, as well as many academics, view a moderate yet constant fall in the purchasing power of money as necessary for prosperity. Deflation is seen as a great evil. Yet in a market economy free from government expansion of the money supply, prices would generally fall over time. People would easily adjust to this new situation. Of course this observation is not a justification for a deliberate, government-engineered fall in prices.

19. THE GOLD STANDARD

Praxeology explains the emergence of money, but it is a task for the historians to explain why gold emerged as the worldwide money. The age of the gold standard marked the hallmark of classical liberalism. Those who view boundless credit expansion as the solution to mankind's problems necessarily hate the gold standard for the discipline it imposes on central banks.

International Monetary Cooperation

No cooperation is necessary to make an international gold standard work. Each government redeems its notes in exchange for the stipulated weight of gold. The various schemes for monetary cooperation are attempts to evade the limits to fiduciary media that a unilateral central bank would experience. If all governments expand in concert, then there will be no drain on their monetary reserves. This approach still overlooks the problem of the trade cycle, dealt with in chapter XX.

Why It Matters

This crucial chapter explains one of Mises's major contributions to economic theory, namely, his regression theorem. It is no overstatement to say that Mises unified micro- and macro-economics with this application of marginal-utility theory to the problem of money. In this chapter, Mises also explains the origin of money, how laissez-faire in banking would work, and hints at his theory of the boom-bust cycle, which will be fully explained in chapter XX.

Technical Notes

(1)   In defending his regression theorem explaining the exchange value of money, Mises writes, "Finally it was objected . . . that its approach is historical, not theoretical" (p. 407). This is an interesting issue, because on the surface it *does* seem as if Mises has deviated from the praxeological approach. After all, doesn't his explanation of the purchasing power of money seem to rely on a historical narrative, much as his archrivals in the German Historical School might give? Yet this is a superficial conclusion. Mises is not delving into history to see how gold in practice actually derived its purchasing power. On the contrary, one can logically follow the regression theorem without looking at any history books. It is a logical, theoretical construction that involves the passage of time.

(2)   In the discussion of free banking (p. 435), Mises alludes to a frequent objection that justifies government intervention on the grounds that ignorant individuals will be helpless to judge the quality of notes issued by unregulated banks. Notice that Mises's defense of free banking works even if everyone initially accepts unfamiliar banknotes. His point is that such recipients will get rid of these notes as quickly as possible, by either spending them or depositing them with their own bank. (The situation is similar to someone today who

has both a $20 bill and a check for $20 written by someone unfamiliar. Which will be deposited at the bank first?) Soon enough these notes will find their way back to the issuing bank.

(3)   The crucial difference between money substitutes and secondary media of exchange are that the latter must first be exchanged against money before their owner can obtain his ultimate objective. (See p. 461.)

(4)   Beyond the distinction mentioned in note 3, there is a very subtle difference between what Mises calls *credit money* (pp. 425–26) and *secondary media of exchange* (pp. 459–60). Both may be claims for units of money against a reputable issuer, such as the government or a respected bank. The difference is that Mises defines credit money as claims that originally were *immediately redeemable*, but for which the redemption has been suspended. Since they are not contractually credit instruments (despite their confusing name), they do not bear interest, though they trade below par because of the possibility that the issuer will never redeem them. In contrast, a secondary medium of exchange such as a government bond is exactly what it purports to be: in this case, a claim for future payment of money. It trades at a premium because of its marketability; i.e., it commands a higher price in the market than it would solely on account of the present value of the expected future cash flows to which its owner is entitled.

Chapter XVII: Indirect Exchange 165

(Note that not all secondary media of exchange are legal claims to money; Mises gives the example of jewels. We focus on bonds in this technical note to distinguish credit money from secondary media of exchange.)

Study Questions

1. MEDIA OF EXCHANGE AND MONEY

- What is indirect exchange? What are media of exchange?

2. OBSERVATIONS ON SOME WIDESPREAD ERRORS

- Why is it erroneous to speak of "neutral money"?

- What's wrong with the equation of exchange?

- Does objective use value influence prices?

- Why is the equation of exchange incompatible with the fundamental principles of economic thought?

3. DEMAND FOR MONEY AND SUPPLY OF MONEY

- What is meant by a more "marketable" good? Does it simply mean a good that has a higher market value?

- What is the only function of money? Is money an economic good?

- What is the definition of a cash holding? Does the term "circulation" make sense under the consideration of cash holdings?

- Why is it erroneous to complain about hoarding? Is there a difference between cash holding and hoarding?

- Why can the appraisement of money be explained in the same way as the appraisement of all other goods?

- What's the confusion behind the objection that the marginal utility for money falls much more slowly than that for other commodities?

- What is Mises's critique of the quantity theory of money?

4. THE DETERMINATION OF THE PURCHASING POWER OF MONEY

- What is the regression theorem?

- Is it necessary to know the immediate past in order to anticipate the future purchasing power of money? In what way does the valuation of money differ from the valuation of vendible goods and services?

- What is the money relation and how does it determine purchasing power?

- Why doesn't an increase in the quantity of money affect the various commodities and services to the same extent at the same date?

- Who benefits from an increase of the quantity of money and who suffers?

- What can we say about the neutralization of cash holdings?

5. **THE PROBLEM OF HUME AND MILL AND THE DRIVING FORCE OF MONEY**

- What is the problem of Hume and Mill?

- Why is it indispensable to stress the fact that money is an economic good and not a kind of numeric value?

Comment: "Money without a driving force of its own would not, as people assume, be a perfect money; it would not be money at all."

6. **CASH-INDUCED AND GOODS-INDUCED CHANGES IN PURCHASING POWER**

- What are goods-induced changes in purchasing power?

- What are cash-induced changes in purchasing power?

- How important is the total quantity of money within an economy?

- Why does government always further the interests of some people at the expense of other groups when it prints new paper money?

- Why aren't the terms "inflation" and "deflation" praxeological concepts?

- What does Mises mean when he states that it "is impossible to fight a policy which you cannot name"?

7. Monetary Calculation and Changes in Purchasing Power

- Why can't economic calculation be perfect? Why is it vain to qualify it as imperfect?

8. The Anticipation of Expected Changes in Purchasing Power

- Is the purchasing power of the immediate past the basis of all judgments concerning money? What is the role of the anticipation of these changes?

- What were the causes of the "flight into real goods" or crackup boom? What is the failure of mathematical economics with regard to this phenomenon?

- What are the different stages of the inflationary process?

9. The Specific Value of Money

- What are commodity and credit money?

- Why can't we make assertions about the size of somebody's cash holding by considering a man's material situation?

10. THE IMPORT OF THE MONEY RELATION

- Can producers be in distress because of a scarcity of money?

- What are the consequences of an inflationary policy?

11. THE MONEY-SUBSTITUTES

- What are money substitutes?

- What is the definition of a money certificate?

- What does *fiduciary media* mean?

- What is the definition of commodity credit?

- What is the definition of circulation credit?

- What distinguishes fiduciary media from money certificates?

- What is the only source of credit expansion?

12. THE LIMITATION ON THE ISSUANCE OF FIDUCIARY MEDIA

- How is confidence important with regard to fiduciary media?

- What is the main argument for each independent bank to issue its own notes?

- What were the consequences of the laws that compelled banks to keep a reserve in a definite ratio of the total amounts of deposits and of banknotes issued?

Chapter XVII: Indirect Exchange　　　　　　　　　　*171*

- What is necessary to prevent any further credit expansion, according to Mises?

- Why do governments profit from using the printing press?

- Why shouldn't we fear a cartel of commercial banks?

- What is the relation between credit expansion and the rate of interest?

13. THE SIZE AND COMPOSITION OF CASH HOLDINGS

- In what way does the employment of money substitutes that are not used abroad fuel the emergence of a surplus? What does surplus mean in this context?

- In which cases does a surplus go abroad?

- What is Gresham's law?

14. BALANCES OF PAYMENTS

- What is the definition of a balance of payments? What information does a balance of payments convey? In what way is the size of the group under consideration important?

15. INTERLOCAL EXCHANGE RATES

Comment: "[A]s a rule commodities move only in one direction . . . [b]ut money is shipped now this way, now that"?

- Why does it make no difference whether the cities concerned belong to the same sovereign nation or to different sovereign nations? What is the role of shipping costs within the frame of these transactions?

- How has government interference sharpened the difference between domestic payment and payment abroad?

- What is the purchasing-power-parity theory? Why does the mutual exchange ratio between various kinds of money tend to a final state?

- Who benefits from dealing with the differences in exchange ratios?

16. INTEREST RATES AND THE MONEY RELATION

- What are the causes for differences in the interest rate?

- Why is it impossible, if A and B are both under the same standard, for the banks of A to expand credit if those of B do not apply the same policy?

- Does some agency need to defend a nation's currency system?

- Can the market rate of interest be permanently lowered by credit expansion?

- What is the only means of keeping a local and national currency permanently at par with gold and foreign exchange?

17. SECONDARY MEDIA OF EXCHANGE

- What are secondary media of exchange?

- What are the most popular secondary media of exchange?

- What is meant by "hot money"? What is its significance?

18. THE INFLATIONIST VIEW OF HISTORY

- What's wrong with the view that economic progress is only possible in a world of rising prices?

- Why will opportunities for earning profit for an entrepreneur appear in a world of falling prices as well as in one of rising prices?

19. THE GOLD STANDARD

- Why is it nonsense to qualify the gold standard as a "barbarous relic"?

- Why did bimetallism, as established by the government, fail?

- Why did governments fight the gold standard?

- In what way does the gold standard limit the field of intervention of governments?

- What are the functions of the International Monetary Fund (IMF)? Is it necessary for the continuation of monetary affairs?

CHAPTER XVIII

ACTION IN THE PASSING OF TIME

Chapter Summary

1. PERSPECTIVE IN THE VALUATION OF TIME PERIODS

All action is directed toward an imagined improvement in future conditions, although some actions are intended to improve the very near future. People do not value fractions of time in the same way. Other things equal, people attach more importance to intervals of time that are nearer in the future compared to those more distant.

There are several concepts related to time that are categories of human action. The *maturing time* is the interval between an action and the fruition of its desired effects; the most obvious example is agriculture. The *working time* is an important feature of action requiring labor. The working time plus maturing time is the *period of production*. The *duration of serviceableness* measures the length of time for which a given action yields an increment in want-satisfaction. The *period of provision* is the portion of the future that an actor seeks to influence.

Action is always oriented to the future. The historical origins of particular capital goods are irrelevant. What matters for action is how to use currently available resources—natural, capital, and labor—to best satisfy future desires.

175

It is an empirical fact that if one lengthens the period of production, the physical yield per unit of input can be increased. This means that if one is willing to wait longer, the productivity of labor and other natural resources can be multiplied. This enhanced yield is counterbalanced by the disutility of waiting.

2. TIME PREFERENCE AS AN ESSENTIAL REQUISITE OF ACTION

Acting man does not value satisfactions and their distribution over time merely in terms of *more* or *less*. Other things equal, a given satisfaction will be preferred sooner rather than later. This rule of *time preference* implies that present goods are more valuable than future goods, if the only difference is their date of availability.

There are obvious psychological and physiological explanations for time preference, but these do not suffice for a praxeological law. The very notion of action implies time preference. If an actor did *not* prefer a given satisfaction sooner rather than later, he would never have a reason to consume in the present moment. He would be willing to postpone consumption until tomorrow, but the next day he would be willing to postpone yet again. Thus to say that an actor wants to consume implies that he has time preference.

In a modern economy a person can refrain from present consumption and earn interest. Even so, people still consume a portion of their income in the present; this is evidence of time preference. The income that is saved for the future is also consistent with the law of time preference, because the positive interest rate (as well as other factors such as relative wealth in the present versus future) render "other things" unequal. The law of time preference doesn't say that everyone must consume as much as possible in the present, only that *the same* good or satisfaction is preferred sooner rather than later.

Observations on the Evolution of the Time-Preference Theory

The classical economists missed the crucial role of time in the explanation of interest, because of their faulty theory of value. The time-preference theory of interest was developed by William Stanley Jevons and especially Eugen von Böhm-Bawerk, and then was refined by Knut Wicksell, Frank Albert Fetter, and Irving Fisher.

Some economists puzzle over apparent counterexamples to the law of time preference. To a person in the dead of winter, wouldn't "future ice" be preferable to "present ice"? However, other things are obviously not equal in these two situations.

3. CAPITAL GOODS

Capital goods are factors of production that have been produced. The first capital goods were necessarily created with the mixture of nature-given factors and labor. Thus capital goods do not represent an independent factor of production. However, it is incorrect to say that capital goods are labor and nature "stored up," for this formulation leaves out the role of time. The owner of a capital good is that much closer to the ultimate goal; if he didn't have the capital good, he would need to first take time to construct it.

Capital goods are the medium through which longer processes are more productive. Human labor and natural resources yield larger output when they are first directed into the construction of capital goods. Capital goods are not only fixed equipment, such as tools, buildings, and machinery, but also "goods in process," such as flour (destined to become bread) and crude oil (destined to become gasoline).

Before lengthening the period of production, a person must first engage in *saving*, i.e., consuming less than what is possible. An obvious example is the stockpiling of consumer goods for the workers who will be devoted to a project (such as construction of a bridge) that will not yield direct benefits for several years.

The structure of production is incredibly complex. At any moment there are countless numbers of overlapping processes using capital goods, handed down from our ancestors, and producing more capital goods in turn. Monetary profit-and-loss calculation gives order to the processes, allowing the owner to determine if his capital (measured by forecasted market prices) is growing or shrinking.

4. PERIOD OF PRODUCTION, WAITING TIME, AND PERIOD OF PROVISION

Action is always forward looking. If one were to attempt to measure the period of production spent in the construction of today's capital goods, this would involve tracing the history of production activities back until the first capital goods were formed. Fortunately, such a computation is irrelevant. What matters is how much time must elapse *now* between the expenditure of scarce factors and the realization of the end sought.

Economics is ultimately about subjective preferences and action, not about physical objects. There is no "objective" way to classify things as capital versus consumption goods; what matters is the role assigned to them by actors. Finished goods ready for enjoyment will be classified as capital goods by an entrepreneur who uses them to feed his workers over the course of time.

At any time, people are using precisely those processes of production that maximize output per unit of input, *subject to the preference for earlier rather than later consumption.* Therefore, if people wish to adopt processes of production that yield more output (or better output) for the same input, they will necessarily have to adopt processes that take longer. If this switch is to

Chapter XVIII: Action in the Passing of Time 179

occur without an interim drop in consumption, there must be a prior act of savings.

The above considerations apply for a given state of technological knowledge. It is true that a new invention or discovery may also allow an increase in output per unit of input, even without incurring additional production time. But even so, once the entire structure of production has adjusted to the discovery of new techniques, it will then still be true that *further* improvements in productivity could be achieved if people were willing to postpone gratification by waiting longer for the finished goods.

The history of civilization is not simply one of ever-greater technical know-how, but also savings and capital accumulation over the generations, which make the labor of present workers far more productive. If a sudden calamity were to eliminate the vast stockpile of tools, machinery, and semifinished goods in process, it would take a very long time for mankind to achieve its former wealth, even though people would know the "state of the art" techniques from the (new) beginning.

Prolongation of the Period of Provision Beyond the Expected Duration of the Actor's Life

All action occurs in the (extended) present, and thus involves present valuations. We can say that *right now* a man values a certain satisfaction that he expects to occur tomorrow more than he values *right now* the same satisfaction not expected to occur for a year.

Of course people can take actions that are intended to benefit other people; the common term for this is altruism. Praxeology can easily handle such actions, for the altruist removes his own uneasiness by helping others. It is also possible for an altruist to wish to help those who will live after he has died, such as his heirs. There is no contradiction here with the law of time preference.

Some Applications of the Time-Preference Theory

The reason the Western nations developed capital-intensive economies is that they adopted the necessary political and legal frameworks of private property under which savings and investment could flourish. Before the First World War, capital was free to move internationally. This allowed the underdeveloped nations a jumpstart in their development, for they in effect borrowed the time embodied in the capital goods being imported from the Western nations. Yet with the rise of Marxist regimes, which "nationalize" foreign investments and corporations, the international capital market is on the verge of collapse. This not only impoverishes all countries, but also sows the seeds for armed conflict.

5. THE CONVERTIBILITY OF CAPITAL GOODS

All capital is embodied in physical capital goods; there is not some idealized, abstract "capital" sum that does not refer to actual capital goods. When a businessman speaks of his total "capital," he means the likely sum of money he could fetch were he to sell all of his capital goods and pay off all of his debts, associated with a particular enterprise.

In contrast to the usual dichotomy between fixed versus free (or circulating) capital, it is more accurate to speak of the degree of convertibility of capital goods. All capital goods are appraised for their expected contribution to a future goal. If new information or a change in preferences alters the overall plan, the capital goods may be devoted to different purposes. The degree of convertibility signifies the ease with which this change in intentions can occur. Generally speaking, the more specific the capital good has become, the less convertible it is. For example, if there is a sudden change in the data of the market, a businessperson will be less likely to regret his purchase of iron than his purchase of iron machine parts.

Chapter XVIII: Action in the Passing of Time   181

Even cash is not a completely "free" form of capital. The owner of cash is also making a judgment about future market conditions; he is not "out of the market." The purchasing power of money could change violently, for example, making the owner regret his "investment" in this particular vehicle.

6. THE INFLUENCE OF THE PAST UPON ACTION

Socialist reformers look at the market economy and see horrible waste. Plants have spare capacity, production and population centers are in unsuitable locations, and factories do not all use the state of the art techniques. Yet what these critics fail to understand is that it is not an arbitrary "bottom line" that prevents the adoption of more productive arrangements, but rather the limited convertibility of capital goods.

It is true, if our ancestors had had our current knowledge, they would have made decisions differently. But we must act now with the capital structure as we have inherited it. It makes perfect economic sense to continue to use "obsolete" factories and equipment if the efficiencies of the newest products do not compensate for their purchase prices. Consumers don't throw out their cars or refrigerators every time a new model becomes available, and the same logic applies to capitalistic production. Even socialist planners would be guided by these considerations, though without market prices they would have no way of knowing whether a particular building should be demolished, or whether a particular factory should be abandoned.

7. ACCUMULATION, MAINTENANCE AND CONSUMPTION OF CAPITAL

The concept of capital is a mental tool. The desire to maintain or increase the level of one's capital really is the desire to maintain or increase the productivity of one's future efforts at want satisfaction. At the same time, capital is always embodied in concrete *capital goods*, which necessarily wear out over time. Thus to maintain one's capital in practice means to successfully anticipate future conditions, in order that the money equivalent of the products of the previous stock of capital goods can be used to purchase anew another stock of capital goods with the same (or higher) total monetary value.

The notion of capital and capital accounting is only meaningful in a market economy, with prices for all of the capital and consumption goods involved. Of course, even in primitive societies, fishermen understood the importance of maintaining their boats and nets in working order. But in a modern economy, with constant changes in technological recipes and consumer demand, reliance on tradition is not enough. Entrepreneurs need market prices in order to determine whether their efforts have increased or decreased their capital.

Additional capital can only be accumulated by saving, which is defined as a surplus of production over consumption. However, this saving need not entail an actual curtailment of consumption, because (for example) natural conditions could have improved, or a technological discovery could have rendered production processes more potent. Even in this case, if some of the additional output is to be devoted to the production of more capital goods, then necessarily consumption must fall short of what it *could* have been. In other words, in order to accumulate more capital goods, it is necessary that scarce resources be diverted away from potential *consumption* goods.

Capital consumption occurs when consumption takes such a large portion of current output that the remainder devoted to new capital goods is insufficient to replace the depreciation of the capital stock. Capital consumption may thus allow for a temporary increase in consumption, but future output is diminished as the stock of capital goods declines.

Chapter XVIII: Action in the Passing of Time 183

8. THE MOBILITY OF THE INVESTOR

Although capital goods have limited convertibility, their owner can avoid impending loss if he foresees disaster and sells them to someone who is less aware of the situation. One must keep in mind, however, that profits and losses emanate from the dedication of scarce factors of production toward ends aimed at satisfying the consumers. The transactions of the stock market do not alter the sum total of these profits or losses, but merely the particular people on whom the profits or losses fall.

These considerations show the futility and pointlessness of foreign-exchange controls. Typically, a government will debase its currency while enacting controls to prevent "capital flight" abroad. Yet this doesn't alter the harm to the domestic economy, it simply prevents the country's citizens from unloading some of the losses onto foreigners.

9. MONEY AND CAPITAL; SAVING AND INVESTMENT

The tremendous advantage of indirect exchange holds in the sphere of capital goods as well as consumption goods; consequently entrepreneurs hold cash balances as well as consumers. Naturally a businessperson will consider his cash holdings (if devoted to his enterprise and not for personal use) as part of his capital, and will add them to the money equivalents of his machinery, equipment, inventory, and so forth. This practice poses a problem for some economists: when calculating the "social capital" of the community, should money be excluded? After all, there is a sense in which one farmer's tractor makes the entire community richer, but it seems illegitimate to count the farmer's $20 bill in his wallet as well.

These paradoxes result from the futile attempt to apply a tool—capital accounting—in a sphere where it doesn't belong. The individual's approach to capital is perfectly correct; cash holdings should be counted as part of capital. The problem occurs when trying to reason from the point of view of society as a whole. It makes no sense to calculate the "total capital value" for all of society, since society will never attempt to sell its entire stock of capital goods to some other buyer. Once we leave the context of an actual market economy with real money prices, we lose the ability to amalgamate heterogeneous capital goods. The capital stock can no longer be reduced to a meaningful number, but is only a collection of different tools, equipment, supplies, and so forth.

Why It Matters

In the beginning of the chapter, Mises explains the important concept of *time preference*, i.e., the desire to achieve satisfaction sooner rather than later. This lays the groundwork for the next chapter's discussion of interest. The modern Austrians differ from most other schools of thought in that they explain interest by reference to subjective time preference, as opposed to the physical productivity of capitalistic production.

For the rest of the chapter, Mises discusses capital goods. Here too the treatment is very "Austrian," because other schools do not emphasize the complex structure of production. Austrian economists stress the limited convertibility of capital goods; once plans change, it is costly to adapt the production structure to the new situation. It is only with this framework that the reader will understand the Misesian theory of the business cycle, to be presented in chapter XX.

Technical Notes

(1) A logical purist might quibble with the placement of the italicized clause in the following quote from Mises:

> Satisfaction of a want in the nearer future is, *other things equal*, preferred to that in the farther distant future. Present goods are more valuable than future goods. (pp. 480–81)

The problem is that the clause is redundant in the first sentence—if other things weren't equal, it wouldn't be the same satisfaction—and is necessary for clarity in the second. A present banana, for example, isn't necessarily preferred to a future banana, because other things might not be equal; a person might have just eaten three bananas in the present, and so would obviously prefer to defer a fourth one for tomorrow.

(2) Mises writes as if the reader is familiar with Böhm-Bawerk's contributions to capital and interest theory (e.g., p. 485). Böhm-Bawerk, the great second-generation Austrian after Carl Menger, wrote an exhaustive taxonomy and critique of interest theories. In particular, he criticized what he called the "naïve productivity theory" of interest, which explained interest as due to the productivity of capital. Böhm-Bawerk showed through argument and clever examples

that this was an insufficient explanation, because if the capitalist had to pay upfront prices for machinery and so forth that fully reflected their expected contributions to the final output at the time of sale, then there would be no margin left over for an interest return. Thus the mere fact that machinery was productive—i.e., that one could produce more with machines than without—was no explanation for a positive rate of interest. Mises followed Frank Fetter in accusing Böhm-Bawerk of ironically lapsing into the same productivity fallacies in his (Böhm-Bawerk's) own explanation of interest.

(3) Mises handles the alleged counterexamples to time preference (pp. 486–87) in a curious manner. All other defenders of the time preference theory deal with the ice-in-winter case as one of different goods due to the subjective experience of the consumer, yet Mises argues that they are "different commodities" by focusing on the technical aspects of turning winter ice into summer ice. When it comes to the miser, the obvious retort is that ends are subjective, and the miser apparently chooses death (in the present!) over eating. Yet rather than give this argument, Mises merely says that these extreme cases "represent a pathological withering away of vital energy," which doesn't make clear why time preference is being satisfied.

(4) Mises discussion of the stock market (pp. 514–17) might cause some readers to think that

he dismissed the importance of this institution, and thought that it had little relation to the "real" economy. On the contrary, Mises once told Murray Rothbard that the sharp line between a heavily regulated market economy and outright socialism was that the former had a functioning stock market. The stock market is crucial in determining who ultimately controls what are often the largest enterprises. In the text, Mises is simply making the point that the ultimate source of profit and loss is not on Wall Street, but rather an outcome of how well or poorly the entrepreneurs devoted factors of production to satisfying consumers. This insight is entirely consistent with the idea that a sophisticated stock market is necessary to ensure that the best people are in charge of the decisions concerning how factors of production will be devoted.

Study Questions

1. **PERSPECTIVE IN THE VALUATION OF TIME PERIODS**

   - Why are the period of production and the duration of serviceableness categories of human action?

   - Why does every choice imply a choice of a period of provision?

   - What are the methods for lengthening the period of provision?

   - What does the choice of a longer period of production imply?

2. **TIME PREFERENCE AS AN ESSENTIAL REQUISITE OF ACTION**

   - Which undeniable fact provides the basis for the concept of time preference?

   - What is the praxeological distinction between capital and income?

   Comment: "We must conceive that a man who does not prefer satisfaction within a nearer period . . . would never achieve consumption and enjoyment at all."

3. **CAPITAL GOODS**

   - What is the role of saving?

Chapter XVIII: Action in the Passing of Time   *189*

- How does time preference restrict the amount of saving and investment?

Comment: "We are better off than earlier generations because we are equipped with the capital goods they have accumulated for us."

- Why did economists err in classifying capital as an independent factor of production?

- Explain why the difference between the price of a capital good and the sum of the prices of the complementary original factors of production required for its reproduction is entirely due to time preference.

4. PERIOD OF PRODUCTION, WAITING TIME, AND PERIOD OF PROVISION

- What is the "Austrian" point of view with regard to technological knowledge and its role in the production process?

- How did foreign capital help poorer nations?

- How does the supply of capital determine the standard of living?

5. THE CONVERTIBILITY OF CAPITAL GOODS

- Why must capital always be in the form of definite capital goods?

- Why can't there be "free" capital?

6. The Influence of the Past Upon Action

- When does it make economic sense to replace an old machine with a new one?

- Why are technological backwardness and economic inferiority two different things?

- What is Mises's critique of the infant-industry argument for tariffs?

- How does the degree of convertibility of the supply of capital goods affect all decisions concerning production and consumption?

7. Accumulation, Maintenance and Consumption of Capital

- Why is capital a praxeological concept? In what way does it differ from the Marxian notion of capital?

- How can capital be accumulated? Why can capital only be accumulated by individuals?

- What is capital consumption?

8. The Mobility of the Investor

- Can capital flight harm the balance of payments?

- Do stock-exchange transactions create profits and losses?

Chapter XVIII: Action in the Passing of Time 191

9. MONEY AND CAPITAL; SAVING AND INVESTMENT

- What happens if an individual saver employs a sum of money directly for the purchase of factors of production? What happens if he employs the additional savings in order to increase his personal cash holding?

- How does hoarding influence the accumulation of capital?

- What are the consequences if fiat money produces the additional units of the individual's cash holding?

CHAPTER XIX

THE RATE OF INTEREST

Chapter Summary

1. THE PHENOMENON OF INTEREST

Originary interest is the discount applied to future goods versus present goods, and is ultimately due to the universal phenomenon of time preference. As chapter XVIII demonstrated, people necessarily value present goods more than comparable future goods. This naturally leads to higher market prices for a given good available immediately, versus an airtight claim to future delivery of the exact same good. This higher market price for the present versus the future good *is* originary interest; it is the phenomenon that the economist must explain.

The classical economists mistakenly attributed interest income (which they called "profit") to a specific class of goods, namely, "capital." They thought interest ("profit") was what "capital" earned, while rent was the type of income earned by land, and wages were the type of income earned by labor. However, modern economics recognizes that rent is a more general phenomenon; it is the income earned by any scarce productive factor. For example, the owner of a snow plow—a capital good—can "rent" out its services, and in a sense even the worker "rents" his services to his employer for a periodic fee. It is also the case that interest is earned not merely by the owners

193

of capital goods, but by the owners of land as well. Someone who pays $100,000 for a parcel of farmland that yields an annual rent of $5,000 would calculate an interest return of 5 percent per annum on his invested financial capital. This is interest income just as surely as that earned by the owner of a factory. As these observations demonstrate, the classical economists were wrong to try to attribute rent and interest ("profit") to specific types of productive factors.

The understanding of the source of interest presented in this chapter shows the fallacy in attempts to explain interest by reference to the productivity of capital goods. It is true that one can produce more output with a machine than without. Yet this technological fact does *not* explain why someone who invests in the machine earns interest. The productivity of the machine explains its price. The machine's productivity per se *cannot* explain why the purchase price is lower than the market price of the extra output that the machine will eventually yield. It is this discount on factors of production (compared to their eventual finished products) that constitutes interest.

2. ORIGINARY INTEREST

Originary interest is not "the price paid for the services of capital," which is the typical definition. The *rental price* of a capital good is due to its services. Interest is not really a price itself, but rather a *ratio* of prices, namely, that of a present good compared to that of a future good.

Originary interest also explains the finite price of land, which (in theory) provides an indefinite flow of services. If people didn't discount income flows expected in future years, then they would be prepared to pay any sum, no matter how high, for a piece of land.

Orthodox treatments will say that the rate of interest is determined in the loan market, by the interplay of supply and

Chapter XIX: The Rate of Interest   195

demand. It is rather the other way around: the willingness to lend or borrow quantities of money at various interest rates is determined by people's subjective time preferences, i.e., by the discount that they place on future versus present consumption. The rate of interest is evident not merely in the loan market, but throughout the entire structure of production, in the "markup" of the price of a finished good compared to the sum of the prices of its inputs. Naturally the "markup" of $100 lent today compared to the $105 paid back in one year must correspond to the markup a capitalist could earn (say) buying ten-year-old wine and selling eleven-year-old wine twelve months later, due account being made for the different risks involved. The same phenomenon of time preference determines the level of markup in both examples; it is not the case that the cash-loan market "sets" or "determines" the rate of interest in other markets.

3. THE HEIGHT OF INTEREST RATES

It is incorrect to say that a higher interest rate draws forth more savings and vice versa. Rather, the discount people place on future goods determines both the amount of saving and the height of interest rates.

The supply of capital goods bears no necessary relationship with the rate of interest. People sometimes assert that capital accumulation leads to lower interest rates, and point to the interest rates in advanced versus backward economies as proof. However, the high loan rates of interest in less-developed countries reflect not merely the pure time discount but also the risk involved in investments in these countries. Although psychology and physiology may suggest rules of thumb regarding income and the amount of saving, these are not praxeological truths and one can always find exceptions.

4. Originary Interest in the Changing Economy

The British classical economists classified the excess of gross revenues over total money expenditures as "profit." Modern economic theory decomposes this difference into implicit wages for the entrepreneur, interest on the capital invested, and true entrepreneurial profit (or loss). If a woman invests $100,000 of her own money into machinery and tools, and also devotes 80 hours of her time per week running her own business, in order to earn a monthly excess of $1,000 in receipts over her outlays, she will certainly not view the business as profitable. She will rightly take into account that she could sell her labor to other employers, and earn interest on her $100,000 by investing it in other ventures, in order to earn much more than $1,000 per month in disposable income.

The distinction between interest and pure profit is evident in the evenly rotating economy, where everything repeats itself day after day. Even in this case, where there is no uncertainty, the sum of expenditures on factors of production is lower than the revenues consumers pay for the finished product. This difference is originary interest, and demonstrates the influence of time preference. Even in the evenly rotating economy, people prefer present to future goods, and that is why the collection of inputs necessary to make a product has a total market value *lower* than the final price for the finished good. Even when there is no uncertainty, it is still necessary to *wait* for the finished product if one starts with the labor, natural resources, and capital goods required for its production. This inherent waiting time is responsible for the "markup" between the prices of a good's inputs compared to the price of the good itself.

In the real world, on top of this pervasive originary interest due to time preference, there is also the entrepreneurial gain (or loss) due to the investor's relatively superior (or inferior) anticipation of future market conditions. The actual rate of interest

Chapter XIX: The Rate of Interest 197

specified in loan contracts, or manifested in the markup between factors of production and the consumer goods they ultimately yield, involves not only originary interest (due to the time involved) but also entrepreneurial profit. This accompaniment of pure profit with every loan or investment illustrates that in the real world, every act is entrepreneurial; people must always forecast future conditions and plan accordingly, knowing that their judgments may be mistaken.

5. THE COMPUTATION OF INTEREST

Entrepreneurs tend to eliminate differences in the originary rate of interest implicit in the factors of production in different sectors. If the markup between wheat and a loaf of bread is higher than the markup between grapes and a bottle of wine, then investors will shift their funds out of wine production and divert them into bread production. (We of course are simplifying the recipes involved for expositional ease.) This shift will immediately drive up the price of wheat and drive down the price of grapes, and will also (perhaps after a lag) drive down the price of bread and drive up the price of wine. The shift will thus shrink the difference in markup between the two sectors. Funds will continue to move until the rate of return in bread production is the same as in wine production.

People necessarily value satisfactions less as they become more and more remote in the future. However, there is no reason for the diminishment in value to proceed at a uniform rate into the future. Indeed, since every actor has a finite period of provision, it is impossible for valuation to diminish in a uniform percentage per time period—because this would mean that each actor places some value (however small) on satisfactions to occur in a billion, trillion, or more years in the future.

It is customary in the loan market to quote interest rates on a per annum basis. This is merely a convention, however, and does not indicate that people discount future time intervals in proportion to their remoteness. The sloped "yield curve"—i.e., the different annual rate of return on loans of varying durations—shows that people do not discount in such an even pattern.

Why It Matters

This relatively short chapter provides the necessary bridge between subjective time preference (the subject of chapter XVIII) and the Misesian theory of the business cycle (the subject of chapter XX). In the present chapter, Mises explains how the discount on future goods leads to originary interest. The chapter will perhaps be one of the most unorthodox for a mainstream economist, because Mises stresses the differences between his understanding of interest versus the standard textbook treatment. In particular, Mises argues that the productivity of capitalistic processes is not the "cause" of interest.

Chapter XIX: The Rate of Interest

Technical Notes

(1) On page 523 Mises writes,

> Originary interest is the ratio of the value assigned to want-satisfaction in the immediate future and the value assigned to want-satisfaction in remoter periods of the future.

Strictly speaking this is nonsensical; as Mises himself explains in earlier sections, one cannot perform arithmetical operations on subjective valuations. What Mises means, of course, is that subjective time preference leads people to value present goods more highly than future goods, which in turn causes the objective market prices of present goods to be higher than those of comparable future goods. The ratio of these prices is the rate of originary interest. For example, if the price of a TV is $110, while the price *right now* for an ironclad claim to the identical TV to be delivered in one year is only $100, then the implicit interest rate is 10 percent. Notice that an investor with $100 could today buy such a claim, wait one year, and then (if conditions haven't changed) sell his mature claim to a now-present TV for $110. The investor has obviously earned 10 percent on his money, and this possibility is due to the fact that people would be willing to pay more for a TV *right now* than for a claim to a TV available after waiting twelve months. It is thus subjective time preference that is necessary and sufficient for positive interest rates.

(2) On pages 524–29, Mises alludes to the understanding of interest shared by Böhm-Bawerk and most modern economists. The mainstream view explains interest by the higher productivity of lengthier production processes. For example, if someone wants to bring water from a stream to his cottage, a very "direct" and quick approach is to use his hands to carry the water. This procedure yields water in the cottage almost immediately, but the volume of water obtained per hour of labor is very small. If the person were willing to postpone the achievement of the goal—namely, water in the cottage—he could greatly multiply the productivity of his labor by adopting a more "roundabout" or "indirect" procedure. For example, rather than using his time cupping his hands and walking back and forth from the stream to the cottage, the person could spend his time finding a coconut and hollowing it out. This would delay the arrival of the first drops of water to the cottage, but (once the capital good had been completed) would greatly enhance the subsequent hours devoted to fetching water. Finally, if the person were willing to wait many months before the achievement of his ultimate objective, he could first construct a pick, shovel, and other tools, in order to dig a trench from the stream to his cottage. This example shows that by lengthening the

Chapter XIX: The Rate of Interest 201

production process, the man can increase the gallons of water in his cottage yielded per day of his labor input.

(3)   On pages 532–33, Mises explains that contractual rates of interest reflect not only pure time preference but also contain an entrepreneurial component. Students of modern financial theory may have difficulty interpreting this statement. When a bank charges a higher interest rate to a borrower with a poor credit history, most analysts would say that this is because of the higher risk involved, whereas Mises (it seems) would say that if the loan is repaid, the higher return reflects the superior judgment of the lender, who forecasted that the borrower would repay when other lenders didn't agree. These subtleties can only be fully resolved in light of the distinction between actuarial risk versus open-ended uncertainty, or what Mises calls class versus case probability (see pp. 107–13). For example, if a bank issues thousands of similar loans to borrowers with poor credit, and charges a rate of interest on each loan such that the rate of return on the entire portfolio (including the defaults) is the same as the overall return from a portfolio of investments in very safe government bonds, Mises probably wouldn't say that the bank earns entrepreneurial profits on all of the personal loans that happen to be repaid, while suffering exactly counterbalancing entrepreneurial losses on the personal loans that ended in default. Rather, he would probably say that the

pooling of the personal loans, and charging a higher contractual rate, removed this quantifiable risk and hence the higher interest rate does not reflect a specific entrepreneurial component. In the same way, an Austrian economist could plausibly argue that the annual fire-insurance premium (for a house that doesn't burn down that year) doesn't reflect pure profit earned by the insurer. Even here, however, if different insurers *disagree* on the likelihood of certain houses burning down, then the revenues received by some of the firms may indeed reflect entrepreneurial profit.

Study Questions

1. THE PHENOMENON OF INTEREST

- What is the definition of originary interest?

- Does the serviceableness of the factors of production explain the interest earned by someone who invests in them? Why not?

2. ORIGINARY INTEREST

- How does originary interest manifest itself in the market economy?

- Why would originary interest exist in a very primitive state of affairs? Is the concept of originary interest still valid in a socialist commonwealth?

- What does scarcity imply with regard to the technological improvement of production processes?

- What are the definitions of plain and capitalist saving?

- What is the essential deficiency of the static system as Schumpeter describes it?

Comment: "If one eliminates the capitalist's role as receiver of interest, one replaces it by the capitalist's role as consumer of capital."

- Can interest be abolished by law? Can interest payments be abolished by law?

3. THE HEIGHT OF INTEREST RATES

Comment: "Changes in the originary rate of interest and in the amount of saving are—other things . . . being equal—two aspects of the same phenomenon."

4. ORIGINARY INTEREST IN THE CHANGING ECONOMY

- What was the British classical meaning of "profit"? What is the modern understanding?

5. THE COMPUTATION OF INTEREST

- Why do the activities of the entrepreneurs tend toward the establishment of a uniform rate of originary interest?

- If a bond is issued with a contractually fixed rate of interest, what happens if conditions change during the life of the bond such that people now discount the future more heavily?

Chapter XX

Interest, Credit Expansion, and the Trade Cycle

Chapter Summary

1. The Problems

The *neutral rate of interest* is the hypothetical, single rate of originary interest—i.e., the rate of markup on consumer goods compared to their factors of production—that would prevail in the imaginary construction of the evenly rotating economy. In the real world, there are different implicit rates of interest in various lines of production, because people cannot perfectly forecast the future.

We recall that money cannot be neutral; changes in the supply of money will not raise all prices uniformly. This driving force of money can influence the determinants of the originary rate of interest, meaning that new infusions of money can redistribute wealth so that the (new) rate of discount on future goods is different from what it was on the eve of the cash infusion. In addition to this influence, however, is a particular disturbance that occurs when new money enters the economy through the loan market. This *credit expansion* is responsible for the trade cycle, or what is now called the business cycle.

205

2. THE ENTREPRENEURIAL COMPONENT IN THE GROSS MARKET RATE OF INTEREST

The actual gross rate of interest quoted in a loan contract reflects not merely the pure rate of originary interest (due to time preference) but also an entrepreneurial component, reflecting the lender's forecast of future conditions. There is no such thing as a truly safe investment. In a sense the lender is a partner with the entrepreneur who borrows his funds.

3. THE PRICE PREMIUM AS A COMPONENT OF THE GROSS MARKET RATE OF INTEREST

If money were neutral, it would be conceivable to imagine a neutral rate of interest, so long as there were no deferred payments. With no deferred payments—i.e., no loans or other contracts stipulating specific sums of money to be paid on future dates—any cash-induced changes in the purchasing power of money would affect all lines of production equally. The entrepreneur who bought wheat in order to sell bread would earn the same gross interest rate as the entrepreneur who bought grapes in order to sell wine, because (assuming the neutrality of money) any sudden change in prices would affect all commodities equally and at the same time.

However, if we allow for deferred payments such as loan contracts, we must assume more than the neutrality of money in order to achieve a neutral interest rate. We must further assume either of the following: (1) the principal of the loan is adjusted with the (uniform) increase or decrease that the neutral money has generated in commodity prices; or (2) the principal does not adjust, but the rate of interest is adjusted by a positive or negative "price premium" to reflect the rising or falling prices. If we make the (unrealistic) assumption of a neutral money, and then supplement it with either of these additional provisions, we can also imagine a neutral rate of interest.

Chapter XX: Interest, Credit Expansion, and the Trade Cycle 207

Of course, in the real world, money cannot be neutral; it has a driving force of its own. Lenders and borrowers naturally do their best to forecast changes in purchasing power. If people generally expect rising prices, the gross market rate of interest will be higher. Yet because additional quantities of money affect particular prices in unpredictable patterns, the adoption of positive (or negative) price premiums cannot produce neutral interest rates.

4. THE LOAN MARKET

At any moment, there are different gross rates of interest implicit in the price structures in various lines. Because people err in their anticipation of the future, entrepreneurs in one branch will earn a higher rate of return than their peers in a different branch. The market process tends to equalize the net rates of interest (i.e., the component of the gross rate that excludes the entrepreneurial component and the price premium) in various lines, bringing them all into conformity with the originary rate of interest, which corresponds to the subjective discount people place on future goods. This equalization is never achieved, however, because during the process new changes occur that move the target, as it were.

As has been demonstrated in previous chapters, market prices enable the entrepreneurs to engage in economic calculation. Those who earn profits have done a better job deploying the scarce means of production toward satisfying the consumers, compared to those entrepreneurs who suffer losses. In this context, the crucial function of the market interest rate is to coordinate the *duration* of production processes. Because of time preference, it makes a difference to the consumers whether the employment of certain resources will yield satisfactions next week, or whether the entrepreneur who uses up these inputs won't be able to deliver consumption goods for several decades.

208   *Study Guide to Human Action*

It is the market interest rate—or more accurately, the whole array of various interest rates on different types of loans—that guides the entrepreneurs in embarking on production processes that correctly reflect both the consumers' patience and the supply of capital goods that previous savings have made available. If people lower their time preference—i.e., if they reduce their discount on future goods—then they will save more and interest rates will fall. At the lower rate, entrepreneurs will find that particular projects are now profitable, and will lengthen the production structure, absorbing the additional savings. When the finished consumer goods finally become available in the future, people will be materially richer, reflecting the higher incomes earned by those who increased their saving at the start of the process. This prosperity is completely sustainable and reflects the general progress of a capitalist society.

However, if the gross market rate of interest is distorted due to changes in the money supply, then this crucial signal may mislead entrepreneurs. In particular, if new money first enters the economy through the loan market, then the gross interest rate will fall and encourage entrepreneurs to expand their activities. This is a mistake on their part, however, because people's time preferences haven't changed and they haven't saved accordingly. The boom that sets in will be unsustainable, and the prosperity will be illusory.

5. THE EFFECTS OF CHANGES IN THE MONEY RELATION UPON ORIGINARY INTEREST

Changes in the supply of and demand for money can have "real" effects, and in particular they can affect the originary rate of interest. Many writers focus on a certain possibility called *forced saving*, in which an infusion of new money redistributes income from a segment of the population who do not save much into the hands of those who have a higher propensity to

Chapter XX: Interest, Credit Expansion, and the Trade Cycle   *209*

save. These writers thus claim that inflating the money supply can have the beneficial consequence of additional "real" savings and capital accumulation.

There are several flaws with this idea. For one thing, it is not a praxeological law, but only a possible historical regularity. A more serious objection is that it ignores the tendency of inflation to cause *capital consumption*, where people are fooled by rising prices into thinking they are wealthier than they really are, and consequently they raise their consumption inappropriately. This illusion can persist temporarily, because resources can be devoted to the production of present goods rather than to maintaining the stock of capital goods. The situation is analogous to a farmer killing his last chickens and frying all of his eggs for a feast because he mistakenly believed there were dozens more hens in the coop.

6. THE GROSS MARKET RATE OF INTEREST AS AFFECTED BY INFLATION AND CREDIT EXPANSION

Although in the long run the influx of additional money into the economy may increase the gross rate of interest, there is no question that it will reduce the rate of interest if the new money first hits the loan market. This of course is exactly the procedure adopted by governments that, for political reasons, wish to lower interest rates and create an atmosphere of prosperity.

If it were not for continual (and indeed increasing) injections of new money into the loan market, the boom period would come to an abrupt end. Once the disturbance had ceased, prices would readjust and entrepreneurs would realize their plans had been overly ambitious. On the other hand, if the banks continually supply ever larger quantities of fiduciary media (i.e., unbacked money) to the loan market, the gross rate of interest can be held below the level corresponding to the rate of originary interest and the proper price premium. Once in motion, the boom feeds on itself, so long as additional injections of credit are forthcoming. The rise in input prices is not viewed with alarm, because consumer prices are rising too, and with cheap financing, the projects still appear profitable.

As a rule, the government or banks stop the credit expansion at some point, and let the bust or depression ensue. However, if they threw caution to the wind and continually injected exponentially growing amounts of credit into the loan market, the boom could not last forever. After all, printing new pieces of paper does not create additional capital goods. If entrepreneurs attempt to lengthen the structure of production even though people have not freed up resources by cutting back on their consumption, at least some of the entrepreneurs will have to abandon their operations before completion. It would be physically impossible to complete them all, given the technology and available resources. Some businesses will shut down, laying off their workers and selling their inventories.

It is a common mistake to refer to this explanation of the trade cycle as an "overinvestment" theory; in reality it is a *mal*-investment theory. The credit expansion that causes the boom does not create additional capital goods, so there is no question of *too much* investment. Rather, what happens is that entrepreneurs improperly deploy the resources that *are* available, such that some of the production processes put into motion will have to be shut down in the future. The entrepreneurs, misled by the artificially low interest rate, behave as a master builder who lays too large a foundation for a house, because his subordinates incorrectly tell him how many bricks and other materials he has available.

Another typical mistake is to equate expansionary credit policies with rising prices. Yet this need not be the case. In an unhampered market economy, the output of goods and services tends to increase year after year, providing a tendency for falling prices. In this context, credit expansion may simply offset this

Chapter XX: Interest, Credit Expansion, and the Trade Cycle   *211*

trend, such that actual prices remain fairly stable. This is what happened during the 1920s in the United States, when conventional price indices indicated "neutral" monetary policy; in fact, the seeds were being sown for a massive bust.

In the same manner, the "impoverishment" of the bust period is relative. It may be the case that per capita income is higher during the "depression" phase than it was on the eve of the boom period. Yet this doesn't prove the beneficial effects of the credit expansion; people would have been even richer had the boom-bust cycle not occurred.

The Alleged Absence of Depressions Under Totalitarian Management

Critics of the market economy allege that the trade cycle is a natural product of capitalism. This claim is false, because (as this chapter demonstrates) it is only government-backed credit expansion that causes the boom period with its necessary bust. In a sense, the critics are right; there is no such thing as a depression in a society where the dictator arranges all economic affairs. He can order all able-bodied workers to report to certain factories day in and day out, and there need be no "unemployed" natural or capital resources as well. However, this is only possible because the dictator has no barometer of success or failure. In a market economy, the bust period signifies the necessary readjustment of the structure of production, in order to best satisfy the desires of consumers. If we drop that goal, then no readjustments are ever necessary.

7. THE GROSS MARKET RATE OF INTEREST AS AFFECTED BY DEFLATION AND CREDIT CONTRACTION

It is also possible to analyze the reverse procedure, where the government or banks artificially reduce the stock of money by draining it from the loan market. For example, if a government wished to raise the purchasing power of its currency (perhaps to restore its old parity with a precious commodity that had prevailed before an inflationary episode), it might issue bonds to the public and then destroy the funds raised. In two respects this would be the opposite of a credit expansion, as it would temporarily raise the gross rate of interest (since the government would be entering the loan market on the demand side) and would tend to lower prices (since a portion of the money supply would be destroyed).

The problem of deflationary credit contraction is not as important as that of inflationary credit expansion. For one thing, it is politically unpopular and so governments do not typically pursue such a policy. Another important difference is that credit contraction has no lasting ill effects; it may temporarily interrupt borrowing and hence production, but once the interference ends, business can resume as usual. This is not the case with an inflationary credit expansion, because during the boom period the capital structure is physically depleted. Real savings and investment must restore it in order for "business as usual" to continue.

The Difference Between Credit Expansion and Simple Inflation

There are cases where the same tools that cause a credit expansion are used as a convenient way for the government to simply inflate the currency. For example, the government might sell bonds to the central bank, which in turn creates additional reserves in order to buy the bonds. This operation would not, by itself, set into motion the trade cycle, because it is just a roundabout way for the government to create new money in order to finance its budget deficit.

8. The Monetary or Circulation Credit Theory of the Trade Cycle

The British Currency School provided a monetary theory of the trade cycle, but made two mistakes. First, it thought only injections of new banknotes could cause the boom period. However, in reality unbacked deposits will have the same effect. Second and more important, the Currency School only analyzed the cycle in terms of one country's banking sector expanding while other banks exercised restraint. This focus mistakenly led them to conclude that the problem was the drain on the expanding country's reserves. They completely missed the issue of the deviation of the market rate of interest from the originary rate.

In an unhampered market based on commodity money, it is theoretically possible that sudden discoveries of gold (for example) could hit the loan market at an early stage and cause a boom-bust cycle. However, there are two reasons that this possibility is insignificant compared to government-engineered credit expansions with unbacked fiduciary media. First, there is no reason for new gold to enter the economy completely through the loan sector. Second and more crucial, it takes real resources to dig up new gold or other commodities. The danger of new money hitting the loan market and falsifying the rate of interest is infinitely greater in the case of printing up banknotes or adding numbers to an electronic record of reserves, which is all that is required for credit expansion with fiat money.

9. The Market Economy as Affected by the Recurrence of the Trade Cycle

Although the boom period is associated with prosperity, while the bust is considered deplorable, things are actually the opposite. It is the boom period in which resources are malinvested and waste occurs, while the depression (or recession) is the necessary readjustment phase to try to make the best of the situation.

The Role Played by Unemployed Factors of Production in the First Stages of a Boom

The apparent benefits of credit expansion seem particularly obvious when the onset of the boom allows unemployed laborers to go back to work, and unused factories to begin humming. Surely it makes sense to put these factors back to work, producing output for consumers! Yet the problem is that these unemployed factors were the hangover from a *previous* boom period.

Although some nonspecific factors of production can be diverted into alternative employment during the readjustment phase (i.e., the recession), there are other factors—particular workers, certain plants, stocks of inventories—that must remain idle, while their owners try to incorporate them into the revised structure of production. In light of the realization that the earlier plans were erroneous (due to the false interest rate), the owners of these idle resources must accept their current situation and do the best they can. Until they lower their asking price to the now-appropriate level, they will not be able to find buyers in the new environment. This harsh experience is necessary in order for these resources to be correctly redeployed in lines that will satisfy the consumers. If, in the midst of this painful readjustment process, a new inflationary credit expansion is set in motion, so that the idle resources can resume in their original lines, this will not have "cured" the problem. Instead it will only prolong the malinvestments that began during the last boom.

The Fallacies of the Nonmonetary Explanations of the Trade Cycle

Even the theories of the boom-bust cycle that rely on "real" factors must assume that there is a credit expansion to allow their story to play out. Thus everyone concedes that an inflationary

Chapter XX: Interest, Credit Expansion, and the Trade Cycle   *215*

credit expansion is necessary for a boom and bust, while some still deny that it is *sufficient*.

The crucial feature of a business cycle is the prevalence of forecasting errors in *general*. In the market economy, there are always entrepreneurs who make mistakes. But the profit-and-loss system tends to weed out those who cannot learn from the past, and reward those who best anticipate the future. Any particular theory of the business cycle based on nonmonetary causes must explain why the entrepreneurs involved are incapable of noticing the pattern, even though the academic has written books on the topic.

Why It Matters

This vital chapter succinctly lays out the Misesian theory of the trade cycle, or what we now call the business or boom-bust cycle. Contrary to popular belief, the trade cycle is not inherent in the free-market economy, but is rather caused by government intervention in the loan market. The injection of unbacked money pushes down interest rates, preventing them from performing their role in regulating the length of production processes. After digesting this chapter, the reader will understand the causes of the business cycle and what policies would prevent its recurrence in the future.

Technical Notes

(1) On pages 542–43 Mises makes a subtle but fascinating observation on the flaws in time-series analyses of interest rates. He writes,

> In arranging time series of the prices of certain primary commodities, empiricism has at least an apparent justification in the fact that the price data dealt with refer to the same physical object. It is a spurious excuse indeed. . . . But in the study of interest rates, even this lame excuse cannot be advanced.

Mises has in mind the following type of observation: If one econometrician assembles the daily "price of oil" from 1990 to 2000, while another econometrician instead studies the daily "prime rate" during the same period, the latter classification relies much more on a priori theory in order to even collect the "raw data." It is fairly objective to say whether something is or is not a barrel of oil conforming to particular specifications; one certainly doesn't need a theory of oil prices in order to do so. But in order to even classify a particular event as the lending of money to a creditworthy borrower—so that it should be included in the "prime rate" series—one must already have an understanding of what motivates people on the loan market.

Chapter XX: Interest, Credit Expansion, and the Trade Cycle 217

(2) On page 568, Mises argues that sometimes the machinery of credit expansion is employed in simple inflation of the money supply, where the government engineers the creation of new paper money in order to buy goods and services (for which its tax revenues are inadequate). One might wonder why the bank's issuance of fiduciary media (needed to buy the government's bonds) doesn't lower the interest rate. The answer is that this increase in the supply of credit is exactly counterbalanced by the government's demand. Now what *is* true is that the resultant market rate of interest is lower than it would have been, *had the government issued the bonds in any event*—absent the money creation, the government's borrowing would have pushed interest rates up, and this increase would have been "correct." But what Mises seems to be arguing is that this procedure (where the bank issues new credit in order to buy the government treasury's bonds) is economically identical to the government simply printing up the new money itself in order to finance its deficit. There is no question that this latter procedure would have no boom-bust effects, but rather would simply cause prices to rise in ripples throughout the economy. An interesting issue is the fact that in the first case, where the government treasury issues bonds to the banking sector, those bonds still exist after the deficit has been covered in the current year; the treasury must ultimately redeem them out of tax revenues (or additional money creation). In the

case where the government itself prints the new money, there are no lasting liabilities. Thus it is not clear whether the two operations really are equivalent in all respects.

(3) On page 570 Mises deals with the "only objection ever raised against the circulation credit theory." In recent decades, however, the most common objection against the Misesian theory of the trade cycle is that it supposedly assumes businesspeople are incapable of learning—ironically the same objection Mises directs toward other theories of the cycle (p. 581). Specifically, modern economists who subscribe to some version of "rational-expectations" theory ask the Austrian, "Why doesn't the business community realize that the gross rate of interest is false? Why do entrepreneurs mechanically plug in the interest rate to compute profitability, rather than studying monetary policies and adjusting their calculations?" Modern Austrians have given several replies. For one thing, it is impossible for businesspeople to perfectly calculate the impact that injections of new money will have; that's Mises's whole point about the driving force of money. In effect, the critics seem to be asking why the entrepreneurs don't perform their calculations with the originary rate of interest, when the crucial point is that they need the market to tell them what it is. A second response is that there is a "prisoner's dilemma" aspect to the situation. If the government is in effect handing out $100 bills to any

Chapter XX: Interest, Credit Expansion, and the Trade Cycle

entrepreneurs who are willing to take them, how could this not disrupt the market for factors of production? Even if everyone is aware that an unsustainable boom is underway, people still benefit from playing along.

Study Questions

1. THE PROBLEMS

- What is the definition of the neutral rate of interest?

- What is the definition of the gross money rate of interest?

2. THE ENTREPRENEURIAL COMPONENT IN THE GROSS MARKET RATE OF INTEREST

- How does the entrepreneurial component in all species of loans manifest itself?

3. THE PRICE PREMIUM AS COMPONENT OF THE GROSS MARKET RATE OF INTEREST

- How do the speculations of the promoters influence the gross market rate of interest?

- Why can't price premiums render the interest rate neutral?

- How do price premiums come into existence?

4. THE LOAN MARKET

- What role does the rate of interest play with regard to business planning?

- How can the supply of money affect the market interest rate? How does it affect the originary rate of interest?

Chapter XX: Interest, Credit Expansion, and the Trade Cycle 221

5. THE EFFECTS OF CHANGES IN THE MONEY RELATION UPON ORIGINARY INTEREST

- What are the consequences of forced saving for originary interest?

- How can inflation provide the illusion of profits?

6. THE GROSS MARKET RATE OF INTEREST AS AFFECTED BY INFLATION AND CREDIT EXPANSION

- How can it be that the German Reichsbank's discount rate of 90 percent was, in the fall of 1923, a low rate?

- In what way can credit expansion create booms? Are they durable? Why are these booms not long lasting?

- How can a general rise in prices occur?

- What are the differences between an artificial boom created by credit expansion and a normal expansion of production with regard to capital goods?

- If one wants to know whether there is an artificial expansion underway, where should one look?

- Why is it important to stress the difference between malinvestment and overinvestment?

- Why do commodity prices not necessarily rise within a period of credit expansion?

7. The Gross Market Rate of Interest as Affected by Deflation and Credit Contraction

- What are the essential consequences of deflation and credit restriction?

8. The Monetary or Circulation Credit Theory of the Trade Cycle

- What are the two shortcomings of the British Currency School, according to Mises?

- Can a new influx of gold create a credit expansion?

9. The Market Economy as Affected by the Recurrence of the Trade Cycle

- Why are there always unsold inventories in the changing economy?

- Can unused capacity justify a credit expansion?

- Can there be a nonmonetary explanation of the trade cycle?

Chapter XXI

Work and Wages

Chapter Summary

1. Introversive Labor and Extroversive Labor

A man may overcome the disutility of labor—which is the same thing as saying he will be willing to forgo the pleasures of leisure—for various reasons, including the following:

(1) He works in order to strengthen his body and mind, for example through weightlifting or study of esoteric subjects.

(2) He endures the disutility of labor out of duty to God. (This is different from category 4 below only if the rewards from such pious service accrue in the afterlife.)

(3) He works in order to avoid greater mischief. For example, cutting the lawn may take his mind off of a divorce and keep him from drinking.

(4) He works because he subjectively values the fruits of the labor more than the leisure he must sacrifice in order to obtain them.

Of the above motivations, 1–3 are examples of *introversive* labor, where the disutility of the labor is a necessary ingredient

224   *Study Guide to Human Action*

of the experience. (Climbing a mountain doesn't become more
satisfactory if one uses a helicopter; that would defeat the whole
purpose.) Only category 4 is *extroversive* labor, which is handled
separately by economics. Introversive labor is actually treated as
consumption in terms of economic theory, even though there
are cases where people who are laboring for its own sake end up
producing marketable products, which then of course influence
market prices.

2. JOY AND TEDIUM OF LABOR

Even within the category of extroversive labor—where
someone seeks the product of the labor, and views the labor
itself as irksome—there can be attendant feelings of joy and
tedium. There are several sources of the joy of labor:

(1)   The anticipation of the eventual fruit of the labor.
       This includes feelings of self-respect for being a
       self-sufficient member of society.

(2)   The worker enjoys the aesthetic appeal of his cre-
       ations; he takes pride in what he has made.

(3)   After the task is completed the worker feels joy in
       having endured the unpleasantness that is now
       finished.

(4)   Certain occupations appeal to idiosyncratic tastes,
       such as sadists who enjoy being prison guards.

The joy and tedium of labor are psychological experiences
that do not affect the disutility of labor, and hence do not alter
the quantities of various types of labor offered on the market.
However, even though workers will still sell the same number
of hours to employers in either case, they are definitely happier
if they view themselves as part of a benign division of labor. In
contrast, if socialist or union propaganda convinces them that

Chapter XXI: Work and Wages   *225*

they are toiling cogs at the mercy of greedy capitalists, then they
will be miserable.

3. WAGES

When someone directly sells his labor to another, the price
paid is called *wages*. Although the seller of labor considers its
disutility, the buyer evaluates labor purely on the basis of its
productivity and usefulness for his own ends. In this sense, labor
is treated as a commodity. There is not one general labor market but rather many markets for labor of different attributes.
Even so, all labor markets are interconnected because an
increase in demand in one branch will draw substitutable workers from related branches, which in turn will reverberate on yet
more remote branches until finally all workers have been
affected by the new data.

An entrepreneur evaluates labor services just as any other
factor of production. He wants to pay as little as possible, but
must compete with other entrepreneurs for scarce labor inputs.
He is willing to pay up to the increment in revenue he anticipates from being able to sell more goods to his own customers,
because of the additional labor he hires. This is what economists mean by saying wage rates are determined by the *marginal
productivity* of labor. If a particular employer paid more than this
rate, he would lose money and eventually go out of business. If
an employer paid less, then his workers would eventually be bid
away by rival firms offering more money (though still less than
the marginal product of the worker).

A typical objection against capitalism is that employers have
an immense bargaining advantage, because the workers will
starve and must accept any wage offered. Yet even if it were true
that all existing employers colluded to restrict wages, this would
offer large profit opportunities for new entrepreneurs to enter
the labor market and bid away workers with slightly higher

wages. Only institutional barriers to entry (typically provided by governments) can allow employers to systematically under-pay workers.

4. CATALLACTIC UNEMPLOYMENT

Despite propaganda to the contrary, workers can and do remain unemployed when they perceive the advantages of available working opportunities to be lower than the leisure that could be enjoyed. On a pure, unhampered market, there will always be some workers who are seeking employment but are waiting for better options to present themselves. This voluntary condition is market-generated or *catallactic unemployment*. There are three types of motivations for such a decision:

(1)   The individual expects a remunerative job in his preferred occupation to become available soon enough, so that moving or finding another line of work are less desirable options.

(2)   The individual works in a seasonal industry and is currently living off of the savings from the periods of high demand.

(3)   The individual cannot accept available positions because they violate his religious, ethical, or social views as to what jobs are proper and which are "beneath" him.

The final wage rate in an unhampered market is that at which all job seekers are able to find work, and all employers are able to find workers, at the given wage; it is the price that equates quantity supplied and demanded on the labor market. In this sense, anyone can get a job in an open market, so long as he is willing to accept the prevailing wage. To the extent that there is unemployment, it is voluntary; potential workers do not

Chapter XXI: Work and Wages

consider the offered wage high enough to compensate for the disutility of the labor.

Changes in wage rates are the mechanism by which consumer sovereignty guides the labor markets. Workers are free to choose whichever occupation they wish, but there must be some way that consumer desires influence their decisions. When consumers shift their demand from one good to another, this eventually lowers the wages offered in the former sector and raises them in the latter. This encouragement of workers to move between sectors is viewed as "coercion" by socialists, but the only alternative is to have authorities decide how many workers should be allocated to various industries.

5. Gross Wage Rates and Net Wage Rates

The employer ultimately cares about the gross payment he makes to his workers, including all benefits (pension contributions, parking spaces, etc.). Consequently if the government mandates that every employer pay a specific portion of Social Security contributions, this burden falls entirely on the worker's take-home pay. Legislated changes in the length of the work week do not make employers willing to pay more than the marginal product when hiring a worker.

6. Wages and Subsistence

The classical economists, misled by their faulty theory of value, explained wage rates as being determined by the bare subsistence requirements of workers. In other words, population would grow until wages just barely allowed workers to buy enough food and other items to replenish their bodies for another day of labor. Among its other flaws, this "iron law of wages" was obviously false, as the standard of living of the average worker continued to grow under capitalism. Later thinkers, including Marxists, adopted the law such that workers' wages

228   *Study Guide to Human Action*

were bid down by ruthless employers until they reached a "socially accepted" minimum level, which could be higher than the bare physiological subsistence. Yet such a historical approach takes wage rates as an external given, and avoids the task of economic theory to explain market prices (including wages) in a complete manner.

A Comparison Between the Historical Explanation of Wage Rates and the Regression Theorem

In a sense, the regression theorem explains the present purchasing power of money with regard to historical facts, namely, the exchange ratios of the money good in the past, when it was either a directly usable commodity itself or (in the case of fiat money) was directly redeemable for a commodity. Even so, the subjectivist theory of money prices still relies on the valuations made today by individuals deciding on their cash balances. In contrast, the Marxist and Prussian Historical Schools explain modern wage rates as *directly* caused by historical precedent; the current valuations of consumers and workers do not enter the explanation. If wage rates are higher in France than in China, this is because they have always been so—not because workers are more productive in France.

7. THE SUPPLY OF LABOR AS AFFECTED BY THE DISUTILITY OF LABOR

Isolated man obviously works until the point at which the benefits of further work are more than offset by the disutility involved. Yet workers in a large market economy follow the same principle. It is true that any individual worker must generally conform to the standards set down by employers, but these standards are themselves the result of the interplay between employers and workers—just as an individual must

Chapter XXI: Work and Wages   229

conform to the train schedule, but the schedule itself is made in order to accommodate the wishes of travelers.

Under capitalism, the accumulation of capital has proceeded more quickly than the increase in population, so that the marginal product of the worker has risen over time. This increase in real wage rates allows the worker to buy more goods and services for a given amount of his labor. His increased wealth may cause him to "spend" more on leisure, meaning that he stops working after fewer hours than his ancestors would have chosen to do. Government and union-mandated "prolabor" reforms are not the cause of the improvement in workers' lots over the 19th and 20th centuries. These changes either codified changes that would have taken place anyway (such as the elimination of child labor) or they hurt the workers by rendering illegal employment contracts that the workers would have preferred to their restricted options.

Remarks About the Popular Interpretation of the "Industrial Revolution"

It is commonplace to romanticize the agrarian lifestyle that existed on the eve of the Industrial Revolution. According to this popular myth, farmers happily farmed the land while women tended to their children. Then the greedy capitalists built their unsanitary factories and packed them not only with starving men but also women and children, and worked them to death. Only the "prolabor" reforms of government and unions ended this horrible exploitation, and yielded the much higher standard of living citizens of Western countries enjoy today.

This fable is completely false. Capitalists had no power to compel workers to enter their factories; the workers did so because they viewed doing so as better than begging on the streets or turning to crime or prostitution. The factory system inaugurated by the new capitalist institutions was vastly more efficient than the medieval guild and manorial system, allowing an explosion of population. Millions of people literally owe their lives to modern capitalism. It is true that working conditions in the 1800s were wretched compared to later times, but improvements were possible only because of capital accumulation, which raised the productivity of labor. The doctrine of exploitation is most clearly exploded by asking *for whom* the factory workers toiled. Mass production creates products for the masses; the landed aristocracy did not buy the entire output of the factories.

8. WAGE RATES AS AFFECTED BY THE VICISSITUDES OF THE MARKET

A worker is born with innate skills and aptitudes that he cannot alter. To the extent the changes in market data influence the wage rates accruing to some skills versus others, the worker either benefits or loses as simple luck, just as the owner of farmland benefits or loses based on the route of a new railroad line over which he has no control.

A worker also can invest in his skills through education, training, and other techniques. In this respect he is a speculator, hoping that the direct monetary expenditures, in addition to forgone leisure and other opportunities during the period of training, are compensated by the higher wages his labor can command because of his enhanced skills.

Generally speaking, unexpected vicissitudes in the market affect the employer's profit margin, not the employee's wages. Of course, once new data become known, they may influence the estimate of a worker's future marginal product and so affect his wages.

9. THE LABOR MARKET

Wage rates are always equal to the price of the "full produce of labor," despite Marxist slogans to the contrary. The workers

Chapter XXI: Work and Wages   *231*

cannot collectively buy the "entire product" because, quite simply, products are made with inputs other than labor.

Although economic theory analyzes the worker as a seller of labor, in the real world a worker is also a consumer. Consequently he may stay in a certain city for "noneconomic" reasons, even though higher wage rates are available elsewhere. In the absence of institutional barriers to migration, wage rates across the world would tend toward the same pay for the "same" labor, but they would not be completely equalized because of this fact. For example, a doctor might be willing to work in Manhattan with a lower standard of living than he could earn in Akron, because he simply enjoys being a New Yorker.

The Work of Animals and of Slaves

People treat animals as means to satisfy their own ends precisely because animals are not capable of engaging in true social cooperation. Yet things are different with humans, because of the higher productivity of the division of labor. Systems of slavery could only survive when propped up with institutional protections, because free labor is so much more productive than slave labor. If a master treats other men as cattle, he cannot expect more than cattlelike performance. It was not moralizing or altruism that ended slavery and serfdom, but the competition from free labor as capitalism swept the Western world.

Why It Matters

In this chapter, Mises explains the supply of and demand for labor, and the principles determining market wage rates. In this respect the analysis is conventional and not idiosyncratically

"Austrian." However, in his historical observations, Mises is very unconventional. He credits the Industrial Revolution with improving the lot of the average worker, and explains that unbridled capitalism—in which labor is bought and sold as a commodity—spelled the doom of slavery.

Chapter XXI: Work and Wages   *233*

Technical Notes

(1)   As with his discussion of the creative genius (pp.
      138–40), Mises here steps outside a more conven-
      tional theory of labor markets in his discussion of
      the joy and tedium of labor (pp. 585-589). In par-
      ticular, his discussion of the "joy of class 4" (p.
      589) is liable to confusion. It is certainly possible
      that the number of people working as garbage
      collectors is lower because of the feelings of dis-
      gust that most have for this occupation. It is true
      that this revulsion drives up wages, and that the
      higher wages counteract the effect of the dirtiness
      of the job. Yet there is no reason that the higher
      wage *completely* offsets the unattractiveness of the
      job; there are probably fewer people working as
      garbage collectors than would be the case if (say)
      people didn't have noses. In the Misesian frame-
      work, then, this aspect of the distaste would be
      classified as part of the disutility of the work
      rather than its tedium.

(2)   Economists often characterize the equilibrium (or
      final) market wage rate as that which allows every-
      one who wants a job (at that wage) to get one (e.g.,
      p. 597). Does this mean that, say, the salary of a
      professional basketball player is too high, because
      clearly there are millions of young men who
      would gladly enter this field and cannot? Obvi-
      ously not. The answer is that the buyer of the var-
      ious units of labor (i.e., the employer) must view

them as interchangeable, according to his subjective valuations. If someone tried to sell a bushel of rotten apples at the market price, he would find no buyer, because his "apples" weren't really units of the same good to which the price referred. His frustration wouldn't indicate a surplus of apples on the market.

(3) Mises says that if workers are "indifferent with regard to their dwelling and working places, there prevails . . . a tendency toward an equalization of wage rates for the same type of work all over the earth" (p. 623). The reader should not misunderstand the claim. Mises is *not* saying that the marginal-productivity theory of wage rates is only approximately true. Suppose autoworkers of the same skill make more in Detroit than in Orlando, because the high crime rate of Detroit deters people from living in the area. Even so, the owner of the factory in Detroit hires workers in accordance with their contribution to his bottom line. If wage rates are higher than they otherwise would be, it is because the smaller supply of available workers has increased their *marginal* product in Detroit factories.

Chapter XXI: Work and Wages

Study Questions

1. **INTROVERSIVE LABOR AND EXTROVERSIVE LABOR**

   - What is meant by "introversive" labor and "extroversive" labor?

2. **JOY AND TEDIUM OF LABOR**

   - Why does catallactics only examine extroversive labor?

   Comment: "Modern capitalism is essentially mass production for the needs of the masses."

   - Why can't ideology affect the disutility of labor?

   Explain: "[N]either the joy nor the tedium of labor can influence the amount of labor offered on the market."

3. **WAGES**

   - What do labor and commodities have in common?

   - How is the height of wage rates determined? How does this differ from market prices for commodities?

   - Why can't the tacit combination among the employers to which Adam Smith referred lower the wage rates below the competitive market rate on an unhampered market?

- Why is it important to stress the fact that the scarcity of labor exceeds the scarcity of most of the primary, nature-given material factors of production?

- Why do wage rates tend toward the marginal product of the kind of labor in question?

4. CATALLACTIC UNEMPLOYMENT

- What is the definition of catallactic unemployment?

Comment: "Unemployment in the unhampered market is always voluntary."

5. GROSS WAGE RATES AND NET WAGE RATES

- What is meant by gross wage rates? In what way are they important for the employer?

6. WAGES AND SUBSISTENCE

- Why is the concept of the "iron law of wages" futile for catallactic reasoning?

- What is the reproach of Mises *vis-à-vis* the analysis of the Prussian Historical School?

- Why are the claims of the labor unions with regard to "take-home wage rates" fallacious?

- What ultimately determines wage rates?

Chapter XXI: Work and Wages   *237*

7. THE SUPPLY OF LABOR AS AFFECTED BY THE DISUTILITY OF LABOR

- Give a short overview of the facts that affect the supply of labor.

- Besides the employer, who can exert social pressure on a worker?

- What is institutional unemployment? What causes it?

- How did capitalism shorten the working hours of workers? How did the proportion between leisure time and working time change?

- Why does a social-security tax always burden the employee and not the employer?

- Why were the laissez-faire economists the pioneers of the unprecedented technological achievements of the last two hundred years, according to Mises?

8. WAGE RATES AS AFFECTED BY THE VICISSITUDES OF THE MARKET

- What is the relation between innate talents and wage rates?

- In what ways does the uncertainty of the future affect the employee?

9. THE LABOR MARKET

- What is the definition of market wage rates?

- Why would workers tend to move from comparatively overpopulated areas to comparatively underpopulated areas?

- Why did servile labor disappear?

- Why is the worker subject to the supremacy of the consumers?

- Does the hired man owe his employer gratitude?

CHAPTER XXII

THE NONHUMAN ORIGINAL FACTORS OF PRODUCTION

Chapter Summary

1. GENERAL OBSERVATIONS CONCERNING THE THEORY OF RENT

The Ricardian treatment of rent was actually quite similar to the marginal-utility analysis of prices; the classical economists were simply wrong in applying the concept of "differential rent" only to parcels of land, and not to every productive factor. More generally, the classical trichotomy of land, labor, and capital—which earned incomes of rent, wages, and profit/interest respectively—was untenable. Although modern economic theory retains these classifications, it uses a single theoretical framework to explain the prices of units of each productive factor. Another major stumbling block for Ricardian economics was its holistic approach. Ricardo tried to explain the distribution of the total output among various classes of inputs, rather than determining the prices (and hence earnings for the sellers) of individual units.

2. THE TIME FACTOR IN LAND UTILIZATION

Modern economics retains the classification of the classical school, and distinguishes first the original from the produced means of production (i.e., capital goods). Then the original means of production are divided into the human (labor) and nonhuman, which is called *land*, though the latter term includes not only parcels of soil but also deposits of tin and schools of tuna fish.

Ricardo wrote of the "indestructible" powers of the soil, but this is irrelevant for acting man. The nonhuman factors of production can be used in ways that preserve their capacity to provide in the future, or they can be aggressively exploited to yield more present goods at the expense of future output. Institutional factors can greatly influence how people treat land at their disposal.

3. THE SUBMARGINAL LAND

A given piece of land can only yield a finite amount of services; that is why land is an economic good, rather than a general condition of the environment. However, the quantity of available land is so large that at any given time, the binding constraint is the scarcity of labor and capital goods available to work the land. This is why people exploit only the most productive parcels of land, giving rise to marginal land that yields no rent (in the Ricardian sense), and submarginal land that is not brought into cultivation at all. An increase in labor or capital goods—even if it were the most unskilled labor, and the least expensive capital goods—would increase total output. Yet an increase in land would only improve humanity's material welfare if the increments were of higher fertility than the marginal land under cultivation.

4. THE LAND AS STANDING ROOM

Some parcels of land must be withdrawn from agricultural or other "productive" uses, to be employed as the foundation for homes, office buildings, factories, and so forth. The high

Chapter XXII: The Nonhuman Original Factors of Production 241

price one must pay for the use of urban land signals the competing uses others place on it.

5. THE PRICES OF LAND

In the evenly rotating economy, the price of a piece of land would be equal to the sum of its future rents, discounted by the rate of interest. Of course in the real world, people make incorrect forecasts, yet their appraisal of land is guided by expectations of its future net yields, whether through agricultural production or apartment rentals.

The Myth of the Soil

Romanticists condemn economists and modern society for treating land as a mere factor of production, rather than a noble source of livelihood and indeed virtue for those tilling the soil. Yet actual peasants do not harbor such notions, which were invented by city dwellers. Those working the land understand that it is a means for the satisfaction of wants, and treat it accordingly.

Why It Matters

In this chapter, Mises explains the determination of both rental and purchase prices for parcels of land. He also explains the evolution of economic thought on the subject.

Technical Notes

(1) The discussion on pages 635–36 explains the "tragedy of the commons," in which people over-utilize a resource (such as a buffalo herd or pasture) because of weakly defined or enforced property rights.

(2) Mises says that in "many countries the owners of land or of certain estates enjoyed special political legal privileges or a great social prestige," and that such "institutions too can play a role in the determination of the prices of land" (p. 640). The distinction between legal privileges and "social prestige" makes it sound as if Mises is adopting the Prussian Historical School's method of explaining certain market prices by reference to custom or social norms. In light of his scathing critique of this approach in reference to wage rates (p. 606), clearly Mises is not saying here that sometimes emotions trump market forces in the determination of land prices on an unhampered market. What he probably means is that, for example, a family of nobility may be willing to pay to keep a particular parcel of land in its state as a hunting ground, in order to entertain guests, rather than sell it for development into a shopping mall. This desire raises the price that developers must pay for other parcels of land.

Chapter XXII: The Nonhuman Original Factors of Production 243

Study Questions

1. **GENERAL OBSERVATIONS CONCERNING THE THEORY OF RENT**

   - Why are land and the services that it renders dealt with in the same way as other factors of production and their services?

   - What is the greatest merit of the Ricardian theory of rent, according to Mises?

2. **THE TIME FACTOR IN LAND UTILIZATION**

   - How is the factor of time important for the utilization of land?

   - Which institutional conditions can affect the utilization of land?

   - Is the assertion that land cannot literally be consumed relevant to the explanation of land as a factor of production?

3. **THE SUBMARGINAL LAND**

   - What is the value of submarginal land?

   - Under which conditions would an increase in the amount of land increase the supply of cereals, etc?

4. **THE LAND AS STANDING ROOM**

   - Is it inefficient to place an apartment building on arable farmland?

5. The Prices of Land

- How do the prices of land differ from those of other factors of production?

- What is the myth of the soil?

CHAPTER XXIII

THE DATA OF THE MARKET

Chapter Summary

1. THE THEORY AND THE DATA

The theorems of praxeology are exact; they are completely true, so long as the conditions they presuppose are present. Praxeology deals with human action as such, and does not concern itself with particulars. The fluctuating data are bodily and psychological features of acting men and women, their desires and value judgments, and the theories, doctrines, and ideologies these actors develop to purposively adjust themselves to their environment. To master the totality of reality, the mind must rely not only on praxeology, but also the understanding of history, which itself relies on the other branches of human knowledge.

2. THE ROLE OF POWER

Contrary to its detractors, economics does not assume that man is "free" in some metaphysical sense. Indeed it is the fact of scarcity—the fact that man is subject to external constraints on his satisfactions—that provides the impetus for action. Broadly conceived, the data of the market include the role that ideologies and coercion have on people's behavior in the marketplace. The theorems of praxeology are all still true in this environment.

3. The Historical Role of War and Conquest

The theorems of catallactics apply whenever there is private ownership of the means of production, and division of labor. The existence of robbers and murderers does not refute catallactics, but merely provides data that influences prices as set on the market. Historically, those conquerors who did not embrace "bourgeois" society faded into insignificance. Plunderers require peaceful entrepreneurs to survive, but the entrepreneurs do not require plunderers.

4. Real Man as a Datum

Economics deals with real men and real actions. Economics does not analyze the behavior of "economic man" or a statistically average man.

5. The Period of Adjustment

The market adjusts to changes in the data, but each change sets in motion a process of adjustment that may take more or less time. The task for entrepreneurs is not merely to anticipate the direction but also the rate of the market's adjustment to new realities. The classical economists systematically studied previously unrealized long-run consequences of government interventions. Economics does not ignore the short run; a long-run analysis necessarily includes the immediate effects of a change.

Chapter XXIII: The Data of the Market 247

6. THE LIMITS OF PROPERTY RIGHTS AND THE PROBLEMS OF EXTERNAL COSTS AND EXTERNAL ECONOMIES

Cases of external costs, or "negative externalities" in modern parlance, do not reflect flaws in private property, but rather loopholes in the legal system. Historically, governments granted polluters and others exemptions from legal action out of a desire to promote industrialization.

The External Economies of Intellectual Creation

An extreme example of external economies is so-called "intellectual property." It is quite possible that without copyright and patent laws, authors and inventors might produce less of their materials. It is beyond the scope of catallactics to recommend where the property rights should be drawn in such matters, however.

Privileges and Quasi-privileges

Legal restrictions on the market economy are not uniformly enforced and respected. If some citizens are exempt from a restriction, this is a privilege. If some citizens simply flout the laws, this is a quasi-privilege. Such cases may lead to monopoly gains or differential rents.

Why It Matters

In this short chapter, Mises explains how abstract, a priori true economic theory can be deployed to explain real actions in the real world. In so doing, he defends proper economic theory (i.e., catallactics) from typical objections. Mises also gives a brief response to the issue of externalities, one of the prime justifications for government intervention given by modern economists.

Technical Notes

(1)   Mises claims that economics "deals with the real actions of real men. Its theorems refer neither to ideal nor to perfect men, neither to the phantom of a fabulous economic man (*homo oeconomicus*) nor to the statistical notion of an average man (*homme moyen*)" (p. 646). What Mises says is true of economics as conceived by Mises, i.e., deductive conclusions drawn from the fact of action. Many other economists did and continue to make such unrealistic models of market behavior, thus justifying some of the criticisms of "economics."

(2)   In similar fashion, Mises denies that economics ignores the short run and studies only the long-run consequences (p. 649). Yet mainstream economists often do construct models and perform "comparative statics" analyses where only the long-run equilibrium outcomes are compared when an element is tweaked.

(3)   Mises argues that government efforts to subsidize activities that yield external economies (i.e., positive externalities) will impair consumer satisfactions, because the tax moneys involved will reduce consumers' ability to purchase items on the market that were profitable before the new taxes were imposed (pp. 654–55). However, a mainstream economist would argue that this "profitability" was spurious precisely because of the positive externality, and that the diversion of more factors of production into the subsidized line increases consumer satisfaction.

Chapter XXIII: The Data of the Market 249

Study Questions

1. THE THEORY AND THE DATA

- Under which conditions are catallactic insights valid?

Comment: "There is no such thing as a mere recording of unadulterated facts apart from any reference to theories."

2. THE ROLE OF POWER

- What determines market phenomena, according to the Historical School?

- Who has the real power in market processes?

3. THE HISTORICAL ROLE OF WAR AND CONQUEST

Comment: "The teachings of catallactics do not refer to a definite epoch of history, but to all actions characterized by the two conditions private ownership of the means of production and division of labor."

- Give an overview of the four points Mises makes in this section.

4. REAL MAN AS A DATUM

Comment: "There is no yardstick that a scientific investigation can apply to human action other than that of the ultimate goals the acting individual wants to realize in embarking upon a definite action."

5. THE PERIOD OF ADJUSTMENT

- What can we say about the period of adjustment? How can we measure it?

- What does Mises think of Keynes's famous phrase "in the long run we shall all be dead"?

6. THE LIMITS OF PROPERTY RIGHTS AND THE PROBLEMS OF EXTERNAL COSTS AND EXTERNAL ECONOMIES

- What is the problem associated with so-called public land?

- What is the difference between the American and the European experiences with forestry?

- Is Mises for or against government grants of patents and copyrights?

CHAPTER XXIV

HARMONY AND CONFLICT OF INTERESTS

Chapter Summary

1. THE ULTIMATE SOURCE OF PROFIT AND LOSS ON THE MARKET

It is not true that one man's profit is another man's loss. In a market economy, those who earn entrepreneurial profits do so by better adjusting production so as to satisfy the desires of the consumers. It is not the existence of disease that generates earnings for doctors, but rather the doctors' (perceived) ability to relieve sickness.

There is no conflict between buyer and seller. Even he who sells at a loss gains from the transaction at that moment. His loss is due to his earlier, faulty forecast; he is grateful that there is now a buyer even at such a "losing" price.

2. THE LIMITATION OF OFFSPRING

Natural scarcity implies pitiless competition. However, with man, the superior productivity of labor reverses this biological tendency; so long as the optimum population has not been reached, additional hands raise the average level of output, making everyone richer. People who understand economics do not

251

view newcomers as strains on scarce resources, but rather as opportunities for intensified division of labor.

The Malthusian law of population is correct as far as it goes, but Malthus and his disciples drew erroneous conclusions from it. Humans do not expand their populations with every increase in sustenance to the point of bare survival. Capitalism leads to declining mortality and birth rates as people purposely limit offspring in order to maintain higher standards of living. The limitation of offspring would be necessary under a socialist commonwealth as well, but here the authorities would make the decisions.

3. THE HARMONY OF THE "RIGHTLY UNDERSTOOD" INTERESTS

There is a harmony of interests, "rightly understood" or "in the long run," among all peoples. A market economy substitutes catallactic competition (which is really cooperation) for biological competition. The fact that most people desire food and shelter does not create conflict over these items, but rather lowers their prices as mass production enjoys economies of scale.

Romantics decry the rise of bourgeois civilization and the loss of a blissful "state of nature." But the overwhelming majority would prefer the comforts of modern capitalism to the backbreaking toil of preindustrial times. Recognizing the tremendous material advantages of the division of labor, man realizes the importance of strengthening social bonds through respecting private property. The workers and capitalists are allies, not enemies.

4. PRIVATE PROPERTY

The institution of private property, where individuals own the means of production, is the essence of the market economy. Catallactics refers to the actual control of physical property, and

Chapter XXIV: Harmony and Conflict of Interests　　　　253

not to legal formalisms. Modern governments have been more or less successful in reducing "private property" to a formal term, with government control growing ever larger.

It is true that all modern property titles can be traced back to acts of appropriation (from unowned nature) or expropriation in the distant past. This is irrelevant, for every day the consumers in a market economy promote and demote owners based on their fulfillment of the consumers' desires.

5. THE CONFLICTS OF OUR AGE

People often describe modern war as the result of "economic causes," especially conflicts between "haves" and "havenots." There is much truth in these claims, but it is always government interference with the market economy that fuels such conflicts. The liberal's solution to war is the respect for private property by governments around the world. If, on the contrary, a government enacts restrictions that hamper the exploitation of its natural or other resources, this imposes genuine hardship on the citizens of other nations. It is vain to hope that international bodies or treaties can prevent armed conflict in such situations.

Why It Matters

In this chapter, Mises emphasizes the peaceful nature of a market economy. It is indeed the basis of civilization, as people learn to view each other as collaborators, not as threats. Ironically, it is the antiliberal policies regarding business that fuel domestic and even international conflicts. People necessarily view each other with suspicion when they believe that one man's gain is another's loss.

Technical Notes

(1) In a free society, people could have as many children as they desired, so long as they paid for their upbringing and other related expenses. The "optimal" number of offspring would be determined in the same way as the "optimal" number of television sets; there would not be a "technical" answer to the problem, but one ultimately stemming from subjective value judgments, informed by market prices. However, the fixed quantities of certain natural resources (including actual land) and the division of labor, interact in such a way that increases in the quantity of workers tends to initially increase average productivity and wages, but after a point leads to reductions in the average standard of living, for a specified level of technological knowledge and stock of capital goods. This is what Mises has in mind when discussing the "optimal" population size (p. 663).

(2) In criticizing socialism, Mises contrasts the productivity argument with the calculation argument (pp. 675–76). This proves that Mises believes there is something qualitatively lost without market prices; it is not simply that output is reduced from what it would have been under private ownership of the means of production.

Chapter XXIV: Harmony and Conflict of Interests 255

Study Questions

1. **THE ULTIMATE SOURCE OF PROFIT AND LOSS ON THE MARKET**

   - What is the Montaigne dogma?

   - What is the ultimate source of profits? What is the source of losses?

   Comment: "There are in the market economy no conflicts between the interests of the buyers and sellers."

2. **THE LIMITATION OF OFFSPRING**

   - What does it mean to "live humanly," according to Mises?

   Comment: "Neither the Slavonic Bolsheviks and nationalists nor their sympathizers in the Indies, in China, and in Japan realize that what their peoples need most is not Western technology, but the social order which in addition to other achievements has generated this technological knowledge. They lack first of all economic freedom and private initiative, entrepreneurs and capitalism. But they look only for engineers and machines."

   Comment: "No foreign aggressor can destroy capitalist civilization if it does not destroy itself."

3. The Harmony of the "Rightly Understood" Interests

- How does Mises view the state of nature?

- What is the source of conflict among humans?

- What is the official social philosophy of Roman Catholicism and of Anglo-Catholicism with regard to the critique of capitalism, at least when Mises was writing?

- What are the two main errors on which all socialist and interventionist authors base their analysis?

4. Private Property

- What does private ownership imply?

- How are the owners determined in a market economy?

- Does the institution of private property have the same significance in an autarkic setting as compared to a social one?

5. The Conflicts of Our Age

- Why wouldn't civil wars and international wars emerge in an unhampered market economy, according to Mises?

Comment: "It is not sovereignty as such that makes for war, but sovereignty of governments not entirely committed to the principles of the market economy."

- Why is economic nationalism incompatible with durable peace?

Part Five—Social Cooperation Without a Market

CHAPTER XXV

THE IMAGINARY CONSTRUCTION OF A SOCIALIST SOCIETY

Chapter Summary

1. THE HISTORICAL ORIGIN OF THE SOCIALIST IDEA

Before the social philosophers of the 18th century laid the foundations of praxeology, writers contrasted the interests of the state and nation against the selfish concerns of individuals. Ironically, it was the classical liberal writers who constructed the imaginary image of an all-powerful and benevolent king. Their purpose was to demonstrate the socially beneficial, spontaneous outcomes of a market economy—which would mirror the outcomes ordered by the good king—but nonetheless they paved the way for calls to install such an actual socialist government to ensure justice.

Historically, there were always calls for an equal redistribution of property, but the rise of modern industry made this impractical. Rather than literal redistribution, the call now came for "socialization" of the means of production. Rather than redistributing the seized property, the state would now handle all economic affairs. Once thinkers ascribed not merely selflessness, but also omniscience, to the state, it seemed barbaric to allow the quaint institution of private property to persist.

257

2. THE SOCIALIST DOCTRINE

Karl Marx did not invent the socialist doctrine. His contributions were the doctrine of polylogism (i.e., the different logical structure of minds of different classes) and the alleged inevitability of socialism. Marx's writings were successful because most thinkers of his age believed in an evolutionary advancement in history, where successive stages are necessarily superior to previous ones. If socialism was inevitable, then it was apparently better than capitalism.

The socialist creed rests upon three dogmas: (1) *Society* is an omnipotent and omniscient being; (2) the coming of socialism is inevitable; and (3) history is a continuous progress from less to more perfect conditions, meaning socialism is desirable.

3. THE PRAXEOLOGICAL CHARACTER OF SOCIALISM

For economics, the crucial feature of socialism is that all productive activities are directed by one will. All workers, all capital goods, and all natural resources are deployed with the sole objective of giving the ruler (or the group of people who collectively run the socialist government) the highest possible satisfaction, according to the ruler's own subjective value scale. The praxeological critique of socialism (to be elaborated in the following chapter) is not over the choice of ends, but whether it is conceivable that socialism can effectively allocate resources to achieve the most desirable outcome from even the dictator's point of view.

Chapter XXV: The Imaginary Construction of a Socialist Society 259

Why It Matters

This chapter provides the historical context for the following chapter, which will lay out Mises's argument for the impossibility of economic calculation under socialism. In the present chapter, Mises explains the true contribution of Marx to the socialist cause, and shows how the classical economists unwittingly aided the socialist theorists.

Technical Notes

(1) Mises describes the insights of the classical economists, including:

> The objectives of entrepreneurship do not differ from those of the perfect king. For this benevolent king too aims at nothing else than such an employment of the means of production that the maximum of consumer satisfaction can be reached. (p. 686)

Yet Mises then criticizes these writers for smuggling in personal value judgments. This is ironic, since Mises too stresses the doctrine of consumer sovereignty. What Mises probably has in mind is that the classical economists did not carefully distinguish positive economic claims (about the true directors in a market economy, etc.) from normative claims (such as the desirability of prosperity, falling infant mortality rates, etc.).

(2) Mises's discussion of the tools at the dictator's disposal (p. 692) is important to clarify the strong nature of his critique (which comes in the following chapter). Mises is *not* merely saying that "in practice" socialism would fail to allocate resources economically. Rather, Mises will make the much stronger claim that, by its very nature, socialist economy is impossible. The problem is much deeper than simply one of dispersed knowledge and other practical obstacles.

Chapter XXV: The Imaginary Construction of a Socialist Society 261

Study Questions

1. **THE HISTORICAL ORIGIN OF THE SOCIALIST IDEA**

   - In what way did old liberals originate the confusion of the perfect state?

   - Why does Mises say, "Every socialist is a disguised dictator"?

2. **THE SOCIALIST DOCTRINE**

   - Why is the coming of socialism inevitable, according to Marx?

   - What is the role of Hegel in the Marxist doctrines?

   - What are the three dogmas of the socialist creed?

3. **THE PRAXEOLOGICAL CHARACTER OF SOCIALISM**

   - What does Mises concede—for the sake of argument—to the socialist dictator, in terms of technical knowledge, obedience of his subjects, and so forth?

   Comment: "Our problem, the crucial and only problem of socialism, is a purely economic problem, and as such refers merely to means and not to ultimate ends."

CHAPTER XXVI

THE IMPOSSIBILITY OF ECONOMIC CALCULATION UNDER SOCIALISM

Chapter Summary

1. THE PROBLEM

To illustrate the central problem of socialism, consider the socialist director who wishes to construct a house. There are many different technical methods that may be used to achieve the construction of a house satisfying prespecified requirements (square footage, etc.). The director may have numerous physical and chemical facts, as relayed by his subordinates. But he cannot reduce these various reports into a common denominator, allowing him to use arithmetic operations. There is no way for him to quantify the cost of each different technologically possible procedure for constructing the house, and thus there is no way for him to construct his desired house while impairing his ability to satisfy other wants to the smallest extent possible.

The paradox of "planning" is that it cannot plan, because the lack of economic calculation means that the planners cannot compare the benefits and costs of a possible use of scarce resources.

2. PAST FAILURES TO CONCEIVE THE PROBLEM

Although a few economists touched on the calculation problem for socialism, they did not stress it, and the insights were

263

264   *Study Guide to Human Action*

lost. It was the mathematical economists who were to blame for this failure to conceive the fundamental problem of socialism. In their formal models, the mathematical economists focus on static-equilibrium states, and so there is no need for entrepreneurship. Furthermore, economic calculation appears possible even without the use of money. This misled many thinkers into believing that socialism was a workable alternative to the private ownership of the means of production.

3. RECENT SUGGESTIONS FOR SOCIALIST ECONOMIC CALCULATION

For much of its history, the socialist theorists neglected the problems of economic calculation. However, the criticisms of economists forced them eventually to offer alleged solutions. All of the schemes are untenable. For example, efforts to value goods based on their inherent labor content ignore the heterogeneity of labor and the contribution of other factors of production. For another example, proposals to value goods according to their units of "utility" fail because utility is an ordinal ranking, not a cardinal quantity that could be measured. (Other suggested schemes are dealt with in the sections below.)

4. TRIAL AND ERROR

The socialist planner cannot resort to trial and error because, without the market test of profit and loss, there are no telltale signs that his plan has been a success or a failure.

5. THE QUASI-MARKET

Initially, the characteristic virtue of socialism was its substitution of one conscious will for the "anarchy" of capitalist production. By replacing the wasteful competition of private ownership with selfless and rational cooperation, the socialists

Chapter XXVI: The Impossibility of Economic Calculation Under Socialism 265

believed they would increase total output and distribute the results according to ethical principles. In light of this historical position, the more recent schemes for "market socialism" are an admission of unconditional defeat. When socialists (conversant with mathematical economics) recommend that planners give instructions to plant managers to behave "as if" they were in a market economy, they concede that the original socialist vision was untenable.

The schemes for socialist citizens to "play market" are as untenable as the original vision. They ignore the fact that under capitalism, the entrepreneurs must decide when and where to *build* plants; the problem is not simply the economical administration of a given factory. Misled by the static-equilibrium solutions of mathematical economics, the socialist theorists advocating a quasi-market concentrate on managerial tasks, and overlook the operations performed in the so-called capital and money markets in a capitalist society.

6. The Differential Equations of Mathematical Economics

Some socialist theorists have suggested that the central planner rely on the tools of mathematical economics to guide his valuation of the means of production. But this too is a vain proposal. The differential equations of mathematical economics describe a long-run stationary equilibrium state. The equations do not shed light on how the planner should take the present world as it is—complete with misallocated capital goods and workers trained in superfluous fields, according to the planner's value scale—and move toward the desired end state, all the while maintaining as satisfactory a condition as possible during the transition phase.

Why It Matters

This is a tremendously important chapter, laying out the impossibility of economic calculation under socialism. Without private ownership of the means of production, there are no market prices for capital goods and other resources. Consequently, the planner cannot calculate the cost—the value of foregone opportunities—of his orders to his subordinates. This is a far more fundamental critique of socialism than the problem of incentives and the possibility of corruption, stressed by previous writers.

Technical Notes

(1) On pages 695–96, Mises concedes that even in a market economy, where entrepreneurs can rely on prices and engage in economic calculation, mistakes are made. However, these mistakes occur because of faulty forecasts of future conditions. In contrast, under socialism, the director has no way of gauging the merits of his planned use of resources, even according to his anticipation of future events at the moment of decision. In a market, people make mistakes, but they at least are made aware of them through the suffering of losses. No such feedback is provided in a socialist arrangement.

(2) On pages 704–05, Mises points out that the quasi-market solution cannot be extended to handle his objection that capitalism is an entrepreneurial system rather than a managerial system. For, even if a socialist theorist suggested that comrades under socialism should be allowed to act in the role of speculators, futures traders, and moneylenders—turning over the profits to the common chest for redistribution—it would be immediately clear that the difference in incentives would render the analogy impossible. One cannot mimic a market speculator if one has no personal wealth at stake and will not enjoy the fruits of one's successes. Moreover, even setting aside the problem of incentives, if the socialist planners really were to endow "socialist capitalists" with such powers, they would

merely be transferring their dictatorship to a different group. The fundamental problem of economic calculation would still remain.

(3) To fully understand Mises's discussion, the reader needs to be conversant with the historical socialist calculation debate. In 1920, Mises published his first exposition of the calculation argument in a German-language article, which he expanded for his 1922 book. In response, many socialist theorists took up Mises's challenge and tried to prove that socialist economy was theoretically possible (though perhaps not practical). The "market-socialism" solution, which instructed the planners to rely on the description of economic efficiency in formal models, was offered by economists such as H.D. Dickinson and Oskar Lange in the 1930s. Friedrich Hayek joined Mises's side in the debate, stressing the practical problems that Dickinson et al. were ignoring in their proposals.

Chapter XXVI: The Impossibility of Economic Calculation Under Socialism 269

Study Questions

1. THE PROBLEM

- Does Mises assume that economic calculation in a market is infallible? Does this affect the validity of his critique of socialism?

Comment: "The paradox of 'planning' is that it cannot plan, because of the absence of economic calculation."

2. PAST FAILURES TO CONCEIVE THE PROBLEM

- How does mathematical economics lend credence to the feasibility of socialism? What is the most significant critique of mathematical economics?

- Why were Soviet Russia and Nazi Germany apparently able to evade the chaos of which Mises warns?

3. RECENT SUGGESTIONS FOR SOCIALIST ECONOMIC CALCULATION

- What are the six suggested solutions for socialist calculation? Give a short overview.

4. TRIAL AND ERROR

- How does the example of searching for a missing wallet relate to the problem with trial and error as a solution to socialist economy?

- Why is it impossible to compare input and output by the methods of arithmetic in a socialist commonwealth?

5. THE QUASI-MARKET

- Why do the new socialist theorists want to keep market institutions intact even if they are in favor of abolishing private property? Why aren't these attempts feasible?

Comment: "The capitalist system is not a managerial system; it is an entrepreneurial system."

- Why is it impossible to *play* investor and speculator? What are the risks that are associated with being a businessperson?

6. THE DIFFERENTIAL EQUATIONS OF MATHEMATICAL ECONOMICS

- What do the equations of mathematical economics describe?

- Why can't these equations provide the necessary information about future conditions? Can these equations be used to determine actions for someone under today's conditions?

- More recent mathematical models in neoclassical economics do not simply describe the long-run equilibrium state. They also can characterize the (equilibrium) transition path to such a steady state. Does this development vitiate Mises's critique of the mathematical approach?

Part Six—The Hampered Market Economy

CHAPTER XXVII

THE GOVERNMENT AND THE MARKET

Chapter Summary

1. THE IDEA OF A THIRD SYSTEM

The systems of market economy and of socialism are neatly distinguished by whether the means of production are privately owned or owned by the government. If the government owns some enterprises but is able to calculate because other companies and capital goods are traded by private citizens, then this is not a "mixed economy" but rather a market economy where some property is owned by the government. Even so, many thinkers desire a system that is neither pure socialism nor pure capitalism—a system that allegedly avoids the evils in both extremes. Economics can inform us whether such a postulated third system can actually work in the fashion its proponents believe.

2. THE INTERVENTION

There are two patterns for the realization of socialism. Under the Lenin or Russian pattern, all enterprises are formally nationalized and become bureaucratic extensions of the state. In contrast, under the Hindenburg or German pattern, the

271

appearance of a market is retained; there are nominal shop-keepers who pay wages and earn revenues, but these numbers are a sham, as all activity is directed by the central authority.

The two patterns are both cases of socialism. The German pattern is not characterized by interventionism, because the government has abolished the market. Under the interventionist approach, the government truly retains the institution of private property, but selectively interferes with outcomes it deems undesirable, using the threat of coercion to alter the actions that would have occurred on an unhampered market.

3. THE DELIMITATION OF GOVERNMENTAL FUNCTIONS

Justice and morality only make sense in the context of society. It is useless to attempt to deduce the "legitimate" functions of government from an analysis of its nature. The purpose of government is to ensure the smooth operation of the market economy by enforcing respect for property rights. Governments obviously have the physical ability to intervene with wage and interest rates in their jurisdictions; the question is whether these measures will achieve their stated objectives.

4. RIGHTEOUSNESS AS THE ULTIMATE STANDARD OF THE INDIVIDUAL'S ACTIONS

Some reformers suggest yet another possible social arrangement, where individuals voluntarily renounce greed and profits in order to satisfy ethical or religious ideals. Such a system, where people are led by conscience and not selfishness, would be neither socialism nor capitalism nor even interventionism (because the government would not enforce the new rules). However, it is not enough to tell entrepreneurs that they must-n't undersell their competitors, or that they must pay reasonable wages to their employees. Once actors in a market are

Chapter XXVII: The Government and the Market 273

instructed to deviate from what they would have otherwise done, the reformers need to be specific in their guidelines.

5. The Meaning of Laissez Faire

In 18th-century France the classical liberals adopted the phrase *laissez faire, laissez passer* to describe their program. They wished to end government interference that crippled successful entrepreneurs from putting their inferior peers out of business. In modern times, "laissez-faire" has come to mean doing nothing in the face of unsatisfactory social conditions. The appeal of "planning" is precisely that it allegedly represents conscious action, as opposed to mindless and "automatic" market processes.

These popular conceptions are completely unfounded. The choice is not between planning or no planning; rather the choice is between allowing individuals the freedom to plan their own lives versus granting all power to the government. If a writer urges the government to overturn a market outcome, this really means that the writer wants armed men to implement the writer's own value system at the expense of the preferences of the consumers.

6. Direct Government Interference with Consumption

If the government directly interferes with the consumption choices of its subjects, catallactics has little to say. Economics deals with price determination by taking the willingness of consumers to spend as a given, without inquiring as to the motivations of this spending. However, in practice governments often attempt to mask their efforts by passing laws not directly on the masses but rather on the entrepreneurs who cater to them. Here is where economics can analyze whether such measures will achieve their stated goals.

274 *Study Guide to Human Action*

Why It Matters

Now that Mises has explained the operation of a market economy, and has demonstrated the infeasibility of socialism, he turns to the suggested third way, namely, a mixed economy that allegedly escapes the evils of either extreme. In this modest chapter, Mises prepares the subject. In subsequent chapters, he will show that this alleged middle path is an unstable, untenable option. The choice still remains for people to choose either capitalism or socialism.

Technical Notes

(1) Although Mises is quite hostile (pp. 716–17) to the idea of natural law—even as deployed by classical liberals whose economic views are quite similar to Mises's—Murray Rothbard and other Misesians were champions of this approach. Rothbard believes that reasoning on the nature of man and his environment can indeed provide guidance to jurists.

(2) In his discussion of proposals for a moral social reform (pp. 719–25), Mises's harsh criticisms may mislead the reader. In an unhampered market economy, people make decisions not simply on the basis of "economic" considerations; people may donate to charities, and employers may retain employees at a monetary loss for nonpecuniary reasons. All of these motivations contribute to the price structure of an unhampered market. But it is precisely this outcome that the reformers do not endorse. Mises's point, then, is that if people are told that their voluntary actions (guided perhaps by Christian teachings) are impermissible, then they must be given specific alternative criteria for their conduct.

(3) In his discussion of direct government interference with consumption (pp. 727–29), Mises says that the prices of goods are dependent on consumer demand, and that the reason for this demand (i.e., whether legitimate consumer preference, or whether government compulsion) is irrelevant. But

under many settings, this distinction would in fact lead to different outcomes. For example, the quality of the products would be different, depending on whether the consumers were purchasing them voluntarily, or were merely forced to by the government. However, Mises is trying to isolate the necessary praxeological flaws with interventionism, and therefore focuses his attention on interventionism's failure to achieve its own stated ends.

Chapter XXVII: The Government and the Market   277

Study Questions

1. **THE IDEA OF A THIRD SYSTEM**

   - What is the third way? What are its characteristics?

2. **THE INTERVENTION**

   - What are the two patterns for the realization of socialism?

   - What distinguishes interventionism from the German pattern of socialism?

   - What does government interference always imply?

   Comment: "The essential feature of government is the enforcement of its decrees by beating, killing, and imprisoning."

3. **THE DELIMITATION OF GOVERNMENTAL FUNCTIONS**

   Comment: "The notion of right and wrong is a human device, a utilitarian precept designed to make social cooperation under the division of labor possible."

   - Does Mises think "Thou shalt not kill" is part of natural law?

4. Righteousness as the Ultimate Standard of the Individual's Actions

- Why would the market economy become a chaotic muddle if the predominance of private property—which the reformers disparage as selfishness—is eliminated?

- What is wrong with the desire for an "altruistic entrepreneur"?

- Why does Mises think the doctrine of just prices and wages would have arrested economic development?

- Why should the sermonizers appeal to consumers, rather than producers?

5. The Meaning of Laissez Faire

- What is the definition of laissez-faire?

- Does the market rely on "automatic" forces?

6. Direct Government Interference with Consumption

Comment: "Every act of government interference with business must indirectly affect consumption."

Comment: "If one abolishes man's freedom to determine his own consumption, one takes all freedoms away."

CHAPTER XXVIII

INTERFERENCE BY TAXATION

Chapter Summary

1. THE NEUTRAL TAX

If the government is to ensure the smooth operation of the market, it requires revenues and these are raised through taxation. We can imagine an evenly rotating economy and supplement it with the assumption of income equality. In such a world, head taxes and income taxes would be equivalent. In the real world, however, these methods of taxation will yield different outcomes. The goal of neutral taxation—where prices are not disturbed by the system of taxation—is unachievable. Every system of taxation will fall on different consumers to a greater or lesser extent, and thus affect market prices.

2. THE TOTAL TAX

Taking the ability-to-pay principle to its extreme, one can imagine a total tax, where the government confiscates either all income or even all wealth, and then distributes it back to its subjects according to ostensibly just rules. As a form of interventionism, the total tax is clearly useless; it either delivers outright

279

socialism, or gives the wealthy the incentive to cease working and consume their capital.

3. FISCAL AND NONFISCAL OBJECTIVES OF TAXATION

The fiscal and nonfiscal objectives of taxation may be in conflict. For example, if taxes on liquor are intended to reduce consumption, the rates may be set so high that total revenue falls. More generally, if tax burdens rise above a certain point, then the taxes cease to be necessary tools for the preservation of the market, and turn into weapons for the destruction of the market.

4. THE THREE CLASSES OF TAX INTERVENTIONISM

The various methods of taxation can be classified into three groups:

(1) The tax aims at totally eliminating or restricting the production of definite commodities.

(2) The tax expropriates a part of income or wealth.

(3) The tax expropriates income and wealth entirely.

The third class is merely a vehicle for the achievement of socialism. The other two classes will be handled in chapters XXIX and XXXII.

Why It Matters

In this short chapter, Mises establishes the categories of tax analysis. He defers much of the specifics to later chapters.

Chapter XXVIII: Interference by Taxation

Technical Notes

(1) In discussing the neutral tax, Mises imagines an evenly rotating economy with income equality (pp. 730–31). It should be stressed that this is an additional assumption; in general there is no need for incomes to be equal in the ERE.

(2) Mises anticipates the "Laffer Curve"—the insight that income tax rates could be so high that they actually reduce tax revenues—in his discussion on pages 733–34.

Study Questions

1. THE NEUTRAL TAX

- What is the definition of the neutral tax?
- Why do governments generally adhere to the ability-to-pay principle in tax policy?

2. THE TOTAL TAX

- What is the definition of the total tax?
- What would be the incentives for the capitalists and entrepreneurs under a total tax?

3. FISCAL AND NONFISCAL OBJECTIVES OF TAXATION

- What distinguishes fiscal objectives from nonfiscal objectives? Give an example.
- How can taxation destroy the market economy?
- How can excessive taxation undermine itself?

4. THE THREE CLASSES OF TAX INTERVENTIONISM

- Give a short overview of the three classes of tax interventionism.

CHAPTER XXIX

RESTRICTION OF PRODUCTION

Chapter Summary

1. THE NATURE OF RESTRICTION

This chapter deals with intentional government efforts to alter production from the pattern that would have emerged on the unhampered market. Its restrictions will also alter the pattern of consumption, but this is a side effect; the goal is to alter production.

Restrictions necessarily make people poorer. On the unhampered market, there prevails a tendency for entrepreneurs to direct resources into those lines that best satisfy the desires of the consumers. If government measures redirect these resources, the consumers are less pleased with the resulting output. Government can only stimulate or encourage particular branches of production by discouraging other branches.

2. THE PRICE OF RESTRICTION

Government restrictions make the consumers poorer, and are thus costly. However, in principle, it is possible that the benefits of the restrictions outweigh their costs, just as one might justify a light tax burden (which admittedly makes citizens poorer) by the military and other government services financed by the tax revenues. However, the typical government restriction is unjustified because it fails to achieve its stated purpose. For example, "prolabor" legislation does not benefit the workers as a class, and "protective" tariffs do not make a country richer.

3. RESTRICTION AS A PRIVILEGE

Although restrictions make the entire nation poorer, each restriction can bestow benefits on a subset of the population. The classic example is a tariff, which reduces per capita consumption but nonetheless provides higher wages to the workers in the protected domestic industry. However, even here the benefits are in the short run only; in the long run, the higher wages attract more workers, until there remains no special boon to working (or investing) in the protected industry. The only permanent effect is a rearrangement of global production so that the product of the industry is produced in regions where its costs are higher than in alternative locations. Despite the fact that everyone is poorer in the long run from restrictions, it is politically difficult to remove them because to do so would cause short-term losses for the privileged group.

One of the major aims of tariffs is to shield domestic industries from the immediate consequences of "progressive" regulation. Under free trade, a new measure requiring employers to revamp their factories would immediately give an advantage to foreign producers suffering no such restriction. But if a tariff is raised to "level the playing field" between heavily regulated domestic industries and their foreign counterparts, then the public cannot so easily see the harmful effects of the regulations.

4. RESTRICTION AS AN ECONOMIC SYSTEM

It is conceivable that the cost of a government restriction—namely, the value of the goods that would have been produced

Chapter XXIX: Restriction of Production   *285*

in its absence, but which now will not be produced—is judged to be acceptable, in light of the benefits. For example, a city government may set aside a piece of land to serve as a park, rather than a site for a factory or shopping mall. Economics cannot say whether the value of the park is higher than the lost output or services from the factory and mall.

However, it is clear that, even when justified, acts of restriction should be classified as quasi-consumption, not as production. Because of this, restrictionism cannot be considered as an economic system.

Various "prolabor" measures do not raise standards of living; they reduce the utilization of a factor of production, labor, and furthermore reduce the effectiveness with which labor can be combined with capital goods. At best, maximum workweeks and other such laws force workers to consume more leisure and produce less output; it is in this sense that the regulations are part of a quasi-consumption program, not a production program.

Why It Matters

In this chapter, Mises drives home the basic yet crucial point that government restrictions on production necessarily reduce the average standard of living. Moreover, even the privileged few who benefit from a given restriction, do so only in the short run. True to his view of economics as a positive science, Mises does not pass value judgment on restrictions. He merely points out that most are ill-suited means to achieve their stated ends.

Technical Notes

(1)   Mises says that the

> decision about each [proposed] restrictive measure is to be made on the ground of a meticulous weighing of the costs to be incurred and the prize to be obtained. No reasonable man could possibly question this rule. (p. 741)

Actually, Mises's disciple Murray Rothbard—certainly reasonable—would question it. There is first the matter of the proper role of government; a believer in the U.S. Constitution, for example, would oppose regulations at the federal level for which there was no authority, even if they appeared to be justified on utilitarian grounds. Furthermore, even taking Mises's argument at face value, one would have to be very careful when weighing the benefits of a proposed regulation. In order to count as a true benefit, it would need to be the case that the unhampered market could not itself deal satisfactorily with the problem. For Mises's example of fire regulations, insurance companies would probably issue codes before granting policies on buildings. In order for government to override these private-sector rules and enforce its own monopoly code, then, the benefit (if any) would have to be due to the superiority of the government's code versus the codes arising in the market; the issue would not be fire codes versus no fire codes.

Chapter XXIX: Restriction of Production 287

(2)   In discussing Americans' importing of foreign goods, Mises says,

> [T]he equivalent of the additional dollars [earned by foreign producers] must finally go to the United States and increase the sales of some American industries. If the Swiss and Chinese do not give away their products [to Americans] as a gift, they must spend these dollars in buying. (p. 746)

Strictly speaking, American imports of foreign goods do not necessarily translate into an outflow of American goods as exports. This is because the Swiss and Chinese can use their dollars not to buy American products or services but instead to buy American assets, such as U.S. government bonds or shares of GM stock. It is true that, in the long run, a country must pay for its imports with its exports; but in any given time period, a net trade deficit can be financed by a net capital surplus, i.e., by foreigners investing more in American assets than Americans invest in foreign assets.

Study Questions

1. THE NATURE OF RESTRICTION

- What does restriction of production imply? What are its necessary consequences?

- What is the only thing that tariffs can achieve?

2. THE PRICE OF RESTRICTION

- What are the consequences of protectionism?

- What are the consequences of restricting the hours of work?

Comment: "Labor legislation, for the most part, merely provided a legal recognition of changes in conditions already consummated by the rapid evolution of business."

- What is the only means suitable to eliminate the deplorable conditions for many Asian workers?

3. RESTRICTION AS A PRIVILEGE

- Why does Mises say "the eagerness of the law's pet children to acquire privileges is insatiable"?

- If each domestic industry is protected by its own tariff, will the move to free trade hurt them all?

Chapter XXIX: Restriction of Production 289

4. RESTRICTION AS AN ECONOMIC SYSTEM

Comment: "Economics does not contend that restriction is a bad system of production. It asserts that it is not at all a system of production but rather a system of quasi-consumption."

CHAPTER XXX

INTERFERENCE WITH THE STRUCTURE OF PRICES

Chapter Summary

1. THE GOVERNMENT AND THE AUTONOMY OF THE MARKET

The government interferes with the structure of the market by enforcing price floors or ceilings that deviate from the levels that would have obtained on an unhampered market. The particular price or wage may have an enforced maximum or minimum, depending on the circumstances and the political strength of the groups involved. Historically, only interest rates have always been subject to ceilings; it has never been politically popular to support the earnings of moneylenders.

If the government imposes controls on all prices, wages, and interest rates, we have socialism of the German pattern. However, many advocates for price control want to retain a market economy; they indeed may claim that only select price controls can prevent the coming of socialism. Economics must inquire whether these programs really can achieve their stated ends.

History is replete with failed attempts at price ceilings and antiusury laws. The failures were always attributed to sinful men and lax enforcement by the authorities. Thinkers in the last centuries of the Middle Ages began to realize there was more to

291

the story, that there were general laws of market phenomena that did not answer to the police power. These laws or regularities in market activity were first discovered in the context of monetary debasement and legal-tender laws, and summarized by Gresham's law ("bad money drives out good," meaning people will hold the genuine coins and trade away the debased ones).

Those interventionists who defy the teachings of the economists regarding price controls deny the existence of economics itself. They cannot admit that there are laws governing market phenomena, independent of men's will, just as there are laws governing nature. Only the insane boast of their defiance of the laws of physics or biology, but governments routinely (try to) defy the laws of economics.

2. THE MARKET'S REACTION TO GOVERNMENT INTERFERENCE

The characteristic feature of market prices is that they equate the quantity of product supplied with the quantity demanded. If the government enforces a maximum price below the market price, there will necessarily be a shortage; buyers will demand more units of the product than sellers wish to supply at the artificial price. Without the use of money to ration the available supply among the potential buyers, other means will have to be used, such as personal connections or even threats of violence. (To avoid these undesirable outcomes, the government often imposes its own alternative system of rationing.) On the other hand, a legal minimum price, set above the level of the unhampered market, will result in a surplus; sellers will supply more of the product than buyers will demand.

Besides these effects, price controls also rearrange the structure of production, and ultimately thwart the intentions of those supporting the controls. For example, the government

Chapter XXX: Interference with the Structure of Prices   *293*

may impose a price ceiling on a food staple, in order to make it more affordable for poor consumers. Yet now capital and labor will flow to other, unregulated industries, because their earnings have been artificially reduced in the targeted industry. Therefore the amount of the food staple being produced is diminished, which is the opposite of the government's aim. The government may try to remedy the situation by imposing price ceilings on the inputs used by producers of the staple, in order to maintain their profitability, but this would simply cause the producers of those inputs to move to other lines. In the end, the government must resort to outright socialism (of the German pattern), or concede that it cannot use intervention to assist consumers of the food staple.

Observations on the Causes of the Decline of Ancient Civilization

The Roman Empire in the 2nd century had reached a high degree of the division of labor. Farmers sold grains and other staples to city dwellers, in exchange for handicrafts and other products made in the cities. However, ever more draconian enforcement of price controls on "essential" foodstuffs, in conjunction with currency debasement, ultimately destroyed the civilization of antiquity and yielded the manorial system of largely autarkic households.

3. MINIMUM WAGE RATES

Governments have generally found it popular to enact minimum floors on wage rates, fixing them at levels above the unhampered market rate. Often the government may defer its use of violence to the exercise of labor unions, which are not punished by the police and courts when they beat "scabs" for crossing picket lines.

294   *Study Guide to Human Action*

If the minimum-wage rates are imposed only on a subset of workers, this will raise the wages of those who remain in the occupation, but drive the rest into other lines (as the employers will choose to hire fewer workers at the higher price). The wage gains of the privileged workers will be matched by reduced wages in the nonunionized sectors. However, if the government or unions succeed in raising wages above their market levels in most or all industries, then the effect is institutional unemployment.

All of the labor-union propaganda overlooks the crucial fact that the only way to raise the average level of wages is to increase the amount of capital per worker. Even the labor unions themselves are dimly aware of this fact, as they have historically sought to exclude immigrants, children, women, and other competitors from the labor force, as well as to oppose the export of capital.

Governments have tried many remedies for the problem of mass unemployment, but each is worse than the disease. Unemployment doles, for example, simply exacerbate the problem by subsidizing leisure; the higher the payment, the less incentive the unemployed have to find jobs. Government spending and public works simply transfer economic activity from the private to the public sphere, where there is no link to consumer satisfaction. Finally, credit expansion can be used in an attempt to trick the workers with illusory nominal pay hikes that do not keep pace with other prices, but the unions will soon adjust their wage demands to compensate for the declining purchasing power of money.

The Catallactic Aspects of Labor Unionism

All that economics needs to stress regarding labor unionism is that widespread efforts to use violence to fix wage rates above their market levels will lead to institutional unemployment.

Chapter XXX: Interference with the Structure of Prices   *295*

When the government abdicates its role as enforcer of property rights and allows unions to exercise such threats, the analysis is the same as if the government itself enforced the wage hikes. The issue is not "freedom of association" or whether workers have a "right to strike"; the issue is whether they should be allowed to threaten violence on strikebreakers who are eager to work at wages lower than the union deems satisfactory.

Why It Matters

This chapter illustrates Mises's view on the only admissible role for the economist to critique government policy: as an economist, one cannot question others' value judgments, but one can point out that proposed measures will not attain the desired ends. Much of this chapter's analysis of price controls' pernicious effects is consistent with standard textbook treatments. However, Mises adds his historical understanding, educating the reader not only on the history of labor unionism but also explaining the fall of the Roman Empire.

Technical Notes

(1) Mises concedes that in very special cases, a price ceiling need not restrict the quantity supplied of a good. He uses the example of apartments in a city: "Thus the amount by which the urban rent of a piece of land exceeds the agricultural rent provides a margin in which rent control can operate without restricting the supply of rental space" (p. 759). Although certainly possible, even here—and especially in a large city—the price control will probably reduce the number of rental units available. Even though the owner of an apartment building won't bulldoze it and plant corn, nonetheless he may be slower in renovating his units, or he may be less aggressive in advertising vacancies, or he may decide to keep some units empty for his own personal storage. At any snapshot in time after the imposition of the rent control, the actual number of apartment units available for tenants would most likely be smaller, even though none of the buildings had been diverted to another use.

(2) The "Ricardo effect" refers to the substitution of machinery for labor when wage rates rise. In general, goods can be produced with varying quantities of workers and capital goods; the cheapest combination for yielding a desired quantity of output will depend on the relative wage rates and rental prices of the services of capital goods. Apologists for labor unions have argued that the Ricardo effect implies

Chapter XXX: Interference with the Structure of Prices 297

that a general increase in wage rates should lead all employers to invest in more machinery, thus raising the productivity of labor and justifying the initial wage increase. Mises points out (pp. 767–70) that labor-union activism cannot increase the quantity of capital goods available to employers; only saving and investment can do that. The Ricardo effect is sensible in isolated cases; a new factory opening in a small town may draw teenage boys from other occupations and raise their wages, which in turn will cause some of the other employers to invest in more "labor-saving" equipment to adjust to the new reality, as they too must pay higher wages to retain those teenage boys who choose to remain with them. But this simply means that such equipment will now be more expensive and redirected from other lines where it would have been channeled were it not for the new factory. In and of itself, the rise in wage rates does not create a larger supply of labor-saving equipment; the increased purchases by the employers in the small town are offset by reduced purchases by other employers, perhaps in other towns.

Study Questions

1. **THE GOVERNMENT AND THE AUTONOMY OF THE MARKET**

   - What does interference with the structure of the market mean?

   - What are the forms of price control?

   Comment: "But the interventionist, in advocating price control, cannot help nullifying the very existence of economics."

   Comment: "The laws of the universe about which physics, biology, and praxeology provide knowledge are independent of the human will . . ."

2. **THE MARKET'S REACTION TO GOVERNMENT INTERFERENCE**

   - What are the consequences if the government establishes

     o a minimum price higher than the market price?

     o a maximum price lower than the market price?

   - If rent control is imposed only on preexisting apartment units, will it have any influence on the supply of new apartments?

Chapter XXX: Interference with the Structure of Prices   *299*

- According to Mises, what are the two exceptions to the rule that price ceilings restrict the quantity supplied of a product?

Comment: "The marvelous civilization of antiquity perished because it did not adjust its moral code and its legal system to the requirements of the market economy. . . . The Roman Empire crumbled to dust because it lacked the spirit of liberalism and free enterprise."

3. MINIMUM WAGE RATES

Comment: "Where there is neither government nor union interference with the labor market, there is only voluntary or catallactic unemployment."

- How can unemployment be voluntary?

- Why does Mises say that Ricardo's proposition and the union doctrine derived from it "turn things upside down"? Why does he think Ricardo has misunderstood the direction of causality?

- Why can real wage rates only rise to the extent that, other things being equal, capital becomes more plentiful?

- Does Mises believe workers have a right to bargain?

- Does Mises approve of measures outlawing unions?

Chapter XXXI

Currency and Credit Manipulation

Chapter Summary

1. The Government and the Currency

Governments do not create money. However, in contractual disputes the courts must determine the meaning of certain phrases, and in this respect all governments must define what is "legal tender." In addition, historically governments have served to certify the weight and fineness of the coins circulating as media of exchange. Many governments eventually abused this privilege by debasing the content of the coins and then passing laws attempting to force their subjects to accept the debased coins at par with legitimate ones.

The international gold standard was the product not of international agreements but of classical liberalism. When governments did not attempt to use their influence on the money stock to achieve other goals, and instead sought merely to ensure the quality of coins circulating as money, the international gold standard and all of its advantages emerged as a happy byproduct.

2. THE INTERVENTIONIST ASPECT OF LEGAL TENDER LEGISLATION

The simplest and oldest variety of monetary interventionism is debasement coupled with legal-tender laws aimed at relieving the plight of debtors. The government inflates the currency so that its purchasing power falls, and then declares that debts contracted before the debasement can be paid off at par with the weaker currency. (Governments sometimes engage in *deflation*, where the stock of money shrinks and its purchasing power increases, which aids creditors at the expense of debtors. But in these situations, the aim was not to help the creditors; this was simply a side effect of the policy.)

As with other forms of interventionism, monetary inflation does not help the debtors in the long run. At best, it provides relief to those with existing debt at the moment of the announced policy. Yet any new debtors will have to pay higher gross interest rates, and if the depreciations occur frequently enough, the credit system may break down altogether. If the goal of the inflationary episodes is to aid debtors, the tool is a failure.

3. THE EVOLUTION OF MODERN METHODS OF CURRENCY MANIPULATION

A metallic currency is not easily subject to government manipulation, because attempts at debasement will lead to the effects described by Gresham's law. In this respect, "hard money" presents an obstacle to government's inflationary aims. The classical economists overlooked this benefit of a hard-money system, when they praised the lower resource costs of using a paper-money system rather than a metallic one.

Under the orthodox or classical gold standard, governments announced the exchange rate between their currency and a specific weight of gold. Subjects carried not only bank notes but

Chapter XXXI: Currency and Credit Manipulation 303

also pieces of gold (often in coins) and spent them as money. Anyone could redeem currency for the appropriate quantity of physical gold. Governments were thus constrained in their creation of additional units of paper money because they could always be redeemed for gold and thus drain the gold reserves of the Treasury.

Under the gold-exchange standard, governments still pledge to redeem currency with specified quantities of gold. However, the public no longer carries gold in its cash holdings; it only holds money substitutes. Furthermore, the government takes steps to dissuade the public from redeeming these notes and thus draining the reserves. By weaning the public from its holding of actual gold in its cash balances, the gold-exchange standard gives the government much more flexibility in inflating the money supply. In fact, the gold-exchange standard as it developed between the world wars was dubbed the *flexible standard* because the pledged redemption ratios between currencies and gold could be adjusted to achieve the governments' aims.

4. THE OBJECTIVES OF CURRENCY DEVALUATION

During the boom period that ended in 1929, labor unions of almost all countries had succeeded in raising wage rates above their market-clearing levels. When the Depression ensued and prices collapsed, the fixed nominal wage rates led to unbearable unemployment. Because they dared not challenge the unions openly, governments resorted to devaluation in order to lower real wage rates without requiring the unions to admit that their demands had been disastrous. (That is to say, with an inflated currency, prices of other goods and services could rise while wage rates remained the same or rose to a smaller extent. This brought them closer to what they would have been without union interference and so reduced the level of institutional unemployment.)

Besides reducing real wage rates, governments also hoped that currency devaluation would achieve the following objectives:

- Raise commodity prices (which would benefit farmers)
- Favor debtors at the expense of creditors
- Encourage exports and reduce imports
- Attract more foreign tourists while discouraging citizens from visiting other countries

Currency devaluation was a poor tool to achieve these ends. Unions learned soon enough to couch their demand in terms of real wages. Aiding farmers with rising prices only punished consumers. Nominal interest rates incorporated a price premium in light of inflation. Finally, the alleged benefits on the balance of trade could only work, even in the short run, if one country devalued its currency more than its trading partners did.

5. CREDIT EXPANSION

Credit expansion can occur even on an unhampered market. Historically, bankers realized that they could profit from maintaining less than 100 percent reserves in the vault, because, during normal operations, most customers would not show up at the same time wishing to withdraw their funds from the bank. However, in an unhampered market where contractual obligations are enforced, the scope of private credit expansion is quite limited.

Things are different in modern times. Governments have seized control of the monetary and banking system, and routinely use systematic credit expansion in the pursuit of various ends. Besides higher prices and wealth redistribution, credit expansion also leads to the boom-bust cycle that plagues modern economies. The gold standard provided a brake on any individual country's credit expansion; if it exceeded the pace of other countries, they would drain its gold reserves. But with the advent of flexible standards that permit frequent devaluations, governments can engage in discretionary credit expansion with much more freedom.

The Chimera of Contracyclical Policies

Socialists and interventionists alike blame recurring depressions on inherent failings of the market economy; they do not recognize the role played by government credit expansion during the boom. Those who advocate contracyclical policies recommend that the government raise interest rates and run budget surpluses during boom periods, and lower interest rates and run budget deficits during economic slumps. What these recommendations overlook is that the slump is caused by a lack of capital goods; during the boom, too many production processes were set in motion and some must be abandoned. The government cannot alter this physical fact through borrowing money or creating additional quantities of paper money.

6. FOREIGN EXCHANGE CONTROL AND BILATERAL EXCHANGE AGREEMENTS

Because of national prestige, and to deny the harmful effects of its inflationary policy, a government may decree a maximum price (quoted in the domestic currency) for units of a foreign currency, which is below the market exchange rate. As with any other price, this leads to a shortage of the foreign currency, because domestic citizens wish to purchase more units of it (with their domestic currency as payment) than foreign citizens wish to sell. This situation is blamed on speculators and an unfavorable trade balance, and is described by the nonsensical phrase "a scarcity of foreign exchange."

The government can resort to makeshifts to ease the problem. It can forbid purchases of the foreign currency except for approved purposes. This may reduce the amount of imports, but in the long run it cannot help the trade balance because the thwarted citizens spend their domestic currency on domestic items, driving up their prices and thus discouraging exports (matching the decline in imports). However "unfavorable" the trade balance was initially, it remains just as unfavorable after the new prohibitions.

The government can enforce the official, overvalued exchange rate, while still permitting the return of the de facto market exchange rate, by subsidizing exporters and taxing importers. Then the interventions on the foreign-exchange market do not alter the conditions of foreign trade, but they do bring the economy closer to full-blown socialism.

In order to conceal the decline in the currency's purchasing power against gold or other currencies, the government may resort to barter agreements with other nations.

Remarks About the Nazi Barter Agreements

The Nazi government of the Reich concluded barter and clearing agreements with various foreign countries. Though these arrangements were heralded as the dawn of a new age in monetary management, in reality they represented ways for the governments to achieve their own political ends at the expense of members of their populations who were out of favor with the government. For example, Germany might agree to trade manufactured goods for farm products with another country, but at prices such that the two collections would be valued at $11 million, even though on the world market each bundle of goods would be worth only $10 million. This would allow Germany's trading partner to bestow a gift on its farmers (who could sell at a higher price than they would have fetched on the world

Chapter XXXI: Currency and Credit Manipulation   *307*

market), and to punish those forced to obtain their foreign manufactured goods through the barter arrangement.

Why It Matters

Here Mises explains why interventionism in the monetary and banking system cannot achieve the popular aims that people believe. As in the previous chapter, Mises supplements standard economic analysis of the issues with his historical understanding. He shows how an initial intervention (with foreign exchange, for example) led to further interventions as the unintended consequences accumulated.

Technical Notes

(1)   Mises writes that

> [o]ne of the main arguments advanced in favor of the flexible standard is that it lowers the rate of interest on the domestic money market. (p. 786)

What he means is that measures to lower the rate of interest through credit expansion will be quickly aborted under a classical gold standard if one country expands more quickly than its peers. However, if the country is allowed to devalue its currency with respect to other currencies and gold, then it can expand credit (and lower domestic interest rates) without fear of a gold outflow. We see this in modern times; when one central bank lowers its interest rate target, its currency generally falls against others in response.

(2)   In discussing the recurrence of trade cycles due to credit expansion, Mises writes,

> It may be that [the businessmen] will avoid using for an expansion of their operations the easy money available because they will keep in mind the inevitable end of the boom. ... But it is too early to make a positive statement. (pp. 791–92)

This is an interesting observation, because the leading neoclassical critique of Misesian business-cycle theory is that he (allegedly) assumes that the

Chapter XXXI: Currency and Credit Manipulation

business community is ignorant of the mechanism. Most modern Austrians deal with this "rational-expectations" objection by arguing that credit expansion is a prisoner's dilemma of sorts, where even if borrowers are fully aware of a credit bubble, the incentives are still rigged to ensure that someone will borrow the cheaper money issued by the central bank.

Study Questions

1. **The Government and the Currency**

   Comment: "A thing becomes money only by virtue of the fact that those exchanging commodities and services commonly use it as a medium of exchange."

   - What were some typical government interventions with regard to currency?

2. **The Interventionist Aspect of Legal Tender Legislation**

   - What is the simplest and oldest variety of monetary interventionism?

   - What are the consequences of debt abatement?

   - Do governments ever engage in debt aggravation? Do they aim to do so?

3. **The Evolution of Modern Methods of Currency Manipulation**

   - Why did the classical gold standard act as a restraint on monetary interventionism?

   - Why were economists—including Mises himself—naïve concerning the gold-exchange standard?

   - What is the definition of devaluation?

- What is meant by the flexible standard?

4. THE OBJECTIVES OF CURRENCY DEVALUATION

- What were the five objectives of devaluation?

- What are the negative consequences of devaluation? Are there positive ones too?

- Can devaluation provide a long-run solution to institutional unemployment?

5. CREDIT EXPANSION

- To what does Mises refer when he says, "The begetter of credit expansion was the banker, not the authority"? What is the situation currently?

- What is meant by "qualitative credit control"?

- What would be the consequences if the credit expansion were limited to special interest groups?

- Is it possible to pursue a credit expansion without affecting stock prices?

- Why is the only real problem to produce more and to consume less in order to increase the stock of capital goods available?

- Why do public-works projects actually intensify the crisis?

312   *Study Guide to Human Action*

6. FOREIGN EXCHANGE CONTROL AND BILATERAL EXCHANGE AGREEMENTS

- What is meant by the term "scarcity of foreign exchange"? Why doesn't Mises endorse this terminology?

- Can governments alleviate an unfavorable trade balance by restricting the imports their citizens can make?

Comment: "The only people who are too dull to grasp what is really going on and let themselves be fooled by the bureaucratic terminology, are the authors of books and articles on new methods of monetary management and on new monetary experience."

CHAPTER XXXII

CONFISCATION AND REDISTRIBUTION

Chapter Summary

1. THE PHILOSOPHY OF CONFISCATION

Contrary to popular belief, under capitalism there is not first a stage of production and then a separate stage of distribution. The two are in fact integrated: as production processes yield their outputs, they are owned by individuals. Acts of outright confiscation may be successful at seizing goods and distributing them to other individuals, but producers will consume their capital if they fear recurrent episodes of confiscation.

2. LAND REFORM

In a market economy, farmland is a factor of production just like any other. Efficiency will bring soil under the control of the most productive farmers, and the size of farms will tend to that which maximizes output per unit of input. If the government interferes with this outcome and, e.g., breaks up larger farms, this will draw people from other occupations into farming. The total amount of farm products will fall, raising their prices. Society will be poorer in order to benefit a few (relatively unproductive) farmers.

3. CONFISCATORY TAXATION

Whether the aim is to raise revenue or to effect social policy, "progressive" income taxation and estate taxes hamper economic growth because they hobble the most productive individuals and provide incentives for the rich to consume their capital before they die. Ironically, the vested interests are sheltered by high marginal rates of taxation because successful newcomers in an industry cannot reinvest their "excessive" profits if the government confiscates them.

Confiscatory Taxation and Risk-Taking

A common objection to confiscatory taxation is that it reduces entrepreneurs' appetite for risk taking: the threat of losses is still the same, but now the government artificially reduces the winnings from a successful gamble.

However, this analysis misconstrues the nature of investment. Investors do not gamble; rather, they place their funds in lines that they believe will earn the most profit. It is impossible to avoid risk taking; if one owns capital, one must decide what to do with it. There are no truly safe investments.

The harmful effects of confiscatory taxation are that they lead to consumption of capital and reduce incentives for further accumulation. The harm is not in rendering capitalists unwilling to engage in risky activities.

Why It Matters

In this short chapter, Mises tackles the popular attitudes toward progressive income taxation and estate taxes. He shows that regardless of their effects on the individuals targeted, they make all of society poorer by shackling the most productive members who can best satisfy the wants of consumers.

Chapter XXXII: Confiscation and Redistribution   *315*

Technical Notes

(1)   When addressing a popular justification for highly progressive income taxes (p. 802), Mises focuses on the effects of such taxes on capital accumulation. However, even on its face, such justifications are wrong because they rely on interpersonal comparisons of utility. It is simply not true that a dollar "means more" to a poor person than to a rich person. We can say that for each individual, the marginal utility of the millionth dollar is lower than that of the thousandth dollar. But this truism cannot allow us to compare the satisfactions of one man to those of another man.

(2)   In his discussion of entrepreneurial risk taking (pp. 805–07), Mises wants to reiterate the point that all entrepreneurial action is speculative; the future is always uncertain; there is no such thing as a "safe" investment. However, one could carefully rephrase the objection against confiscatory taxation in a manner consistent with these insights. For example, a vendor might prepare a large variety of products, hoping to satisfy his customers, whose appetites may be varied. With low rates of taxation, the vendor can afford to offer a wider spectrum of items, because the "hits" will more than cover the expenses of the "flops." But at high rates of taxation, the vendor may instead offer a more conservative product

line, catering to known tastes. It seems appropriate to describe the taxation in this scenario as impairing the vendor's appetite for risk taking, and thereby reducing consumer satisfaction.

Study Questions

1. THE PHILOSOPHY OF CONFISCATION

- Why doesn't the alleged dualism of two processes—that of production and that of distribution—exist in a market economy?

- How does expropriation affect the accumulation of capital?

2. LAND REFORM

- What is meant by agrarian socialism? What objection does Mises have to this term?

- What are the unavoidable consequences of government interference with regard to land?

3. CONFISCATORY TAXATION

- Why is discriminatory taxation really just a mode of disguised expropriation of the successful capitalists and entrepreneurs? Why is it incompatible with the free-market economy? What are its consequences for the accumulation of capital?

- Does confiscatory taxation affect only the rich?

- What is ironic about the interventionists' complaints about the rigidity of big business?

- Does Mises view profits as a reward for risk taking?

Chapter XXXIII

Syndicalism and Corporativism

Chapter Summary

1. The Syndicalist Idea

Syndicalism can mean two different things. First, it can refer to revolutionary tactics used to achieve socialism. Rather than falling for the bourgeois catchwords of liberty, democracy, etc., labor unions should instead use violence to overthrow the capitalist institutions.

A second meaning of syndicalism refers to a method of economic organization. Rather than the socialist goal of government ownership over the means of production, syndicalism in this sense aims at giving workers ownership over their plants and equipment. It is epitomized in slogans such as, "The railroads to the railroadmen," and, "The mines to the miners."

2. The Fallacies of Syndicalism

The root of the syndicalist idea is the mistaken belief that entrepreneurs and capitalists are analogous to kings and aristocrats. The syndicalists believe that "industrial democracy" must give economic power to the workers, just as political democracy enfranchised the people. In reality, the market is a consumers' democracy, which the syndicalists wish to replace with a producers' democracy. This would be a foolish substitution, because the sole purpose of production is consumption.

If the entrepreneurs seem coldhearted to the syndicalists, this is only because the consumers themselves are merciless in how they spend their money. If consumers are not prepared to pay more for goods when the workers have large families to support, then the employers cannot afford to do so either.

The syndicalists rely on a static conception of the structure of production. They overlook the crucial role that entrepreneurs play in the allocation of capital among branches of production in determining which industries shall expand and which shall contract.

3. Syndicalist Elements in Popular Policies

The essence of syndicalist policies is to grant privileges to a minority of workers that result in a lower standard of living for the immense majority. For example, union restrictions may raise wages of a particular group of workers, but they lower wages for excluded workers and lead to higher prices for consumers. Other proposals call for "profit sharing" or even the outright abolition of "unearned income."

4. Guild Socialism and Corporativism

The ideas of guild socialism and corporativism grew out of the desire of the socialists in both Great Britain and Italy to distinguish themselves from the Germans and Marxists, respectively. They drew on the writings of the eulogists of medieval institutions, who praised the guilds as a superior form of organization compared to the wage slavery of capitalism.

The fundamental idea of both guild socialism and corporativism is that each branch of business forms a monopolistic body, the guild or *corporazione*. The entity enjoys full autonomy

Chapter XXXIII: Syndicalism and Corporativism   *321*

to determine internal affairs, such as working hours, technological conditions, and the quality of its products. The guilds bargain with each other directly, and the state is only involved when such mutual agreements cannot be reached.

The essential flaw in this scheme is that entire branches of production cannot be "autonomous" under the division of labor. If the coal miners restrict their hours and raise their wages, this necessarily hurts everyone else in society. It was naïve to think that the vast majority would vest such power in the respective guilds. In practice, guild socialism will revert to outright socialism.

Why It Matters

In this short chapter, Mises deals with guild socialism and corporativism, two related attempts to enjoy the blessings of freedom while avoiding the alleged evils of the anarchy of production. After explaining the historical origins of the schemes, Mises shows that they fail to account for the interdependence of all branches of production under the division of labor. There must be some way to communicate the desires of consumers to the workers in each branch of production. If the voluntary mechanism of the market is rejected, the coercion of the state will be used.

Technical Notes

(1) Mises refers to calls for "industrial democracy" (p. 809). The political climate of his times sheds light on Mises's emphasis on "consumer sovereignty," even though later his follower Murray Rothbard would reject the term.

(2) Again and again, Mises points out that the enemies of the market economy rely on a static worldview (e.g., p. 810). They take the distribution of factories, supply chains, and technological methods as given. They fail to appreciate the essential role of entrepreneurship and economic calculation in determining where to invest new savings.

Chapter XXXIII: Syndicalism and Corporativism   *323*

Study Questions

1. THE SYNDICALIST IDEA

- What are the two meanings of syndicalism?

2. THE FALLACIES OF SYNDICALISM

- Why aren't entrepreneurs and capitalists irresponsible autocrats? Who should the syndicalists blame instead?

Comment: "They are like patients who grudge the doctor his success in curing them of a malady."

3. SYNDICALIST ELEMENTS IN POPULAR POLICIES

- What is the essence of syndicalist policies?

- What are the fallacies of the "ability-to-pay" proposals?

Comment: "If one wants to abolish what is called 'unearned income,' one must adopt socialism."

4. GUILD SOCIALISM AND CORPORATIVISM

- What is the fundamental idea of corporativism and guild socialism? Did Italy realize the corporativist utopia?

Comment: "There is in the scheme of guild socialism and corporativism nothing that would take into account the fact that the only purpose of production is consumption. Things are turned upside down. Production becomes an end in itself."

CHAPTER XXXIV

THE ECONOMICS OF WAR

Chapter Summary

1. TOTAL WAR

The market economy involves peaceful cooperation. The division of labor cannot function effectively amidst a war. Warfare among primitive tribes did not suffer this drawback because the warring parties had not been engaged in trade before the hostilities. Thus they engaged in total war.

Things were different in Europe (before the French Revolution) when military, financial, and political circumstances produced limited warfare. Wars were generally waged by small armies of professional soldiers, who generally did not involve noncombatants or their property. In this context, philosophers concluded that, because the citizens only suffered from warfare, the way to eliminate war was to dethrone the despots. The spread of democracy, many thought, would coincide with ever-lasting peace.

What these thinkers overlooked was that it is only democratic *liberalism* that ensures peace. In modern times, states wage total war against each other because interventionism and central planning lead to genuine conflict between citizens of rival states. Under classical liberalism, political boundaries are irrelevant; free trade and free mobility of labor mean that one's standard of living is unaffected by territorial expansion. Yet under national socialism (and the interventionism of their neighbors), the citizens of Nazi Germany really stood to materially gain from conquest.

Ultimately, treaties and international organizations cannot ensure world peace. Only a widespread adoption of liberal policies will end war.

2. WAR AND THE MARKET ECONOMY

It is a widespread myth that the market economy may be tolerated in peacetime, but in emergency situations—such as a war—the government must seize control of production. During war, resources that normally go into consumer goods must be diverted into products for the military; private consumption must fall. Entrepreneurs can most efficiently effect this switch if they are allowed to earn profits and cater to the new demand, emanating from the government as it spends funds on military items. Whether the government raises its revenues from higher taxes, increased borrowing, or even inflation, in the end the citizens will have less purchasing power, and their reduced consumption frees up the real resources to produce items for the war effort.

In the United States during the Second World War, this process was short-circuited because the government clung to the union doctrine that the workers' real take-home pay must not be allowed to fall, even during wartime. Consequently, the government was reluctant to levy higher taxes, and it imposed price controls to prevent "war profiteering." Given these realities, the only solution was to further intervene in the market, by imposing rationing schemes and other controls, designed to ensure an adequate flow of resources into the war industries.

Chapter XXXIV: The Economics of War   *327*

Modern wars are won with materiél. Capitalist countries defeat their socialist rivals because private entrepreneurs are more efficient in churning out products, whether consumer goods during peacetime or weapons for their governments. Even so, ultimately war and the market economy are incompatible, as the market relies on peaceful cooperation.

3. WAR AND AUTARKY

If a tailor and baker go to war with each other, it is significant that the baker can wait longer for a new suit than the tailor can go without bread. In analogous fashion, Germany lost both world wars because it could not blockade Great Britain, nor could it maintain its own maritime supply lines.

The German militarists were aware of their vulnerability and so stressed the need for centrally planned autarky. They placed their hopes in *Ersatz*, the substitute, a replacement that was either of inferior quality, higher cost, or both, compared to what the unfettered market would have imported from abroad. Yet the inferiority of ersatz items is not a relic of the capitalist mind. Poorly equipped soldiers will fare worse against armies using the most advantageous materials, and higher costs of production mean that fewer finished goods can be produced from given resources.

4. THE FUTILITY OF WAR

Interventionism generates economic nationalism, which in turn generates bellicosity. This tendency is internally consistent; only laissez-faire policies are consistent with durable peace.

328   *Study Guide to Human Action*

Why It Matters

In this short chapter, Mises deploys his skill not only as an economist but also as a military historian. Contrary to popular belief, government controls do not enhance a country's military prowess. Entrepreneurs are more efficient than central planners in the production of tanks as well as the production of television sets. In the long run, however, the market economy relies on the division of labor, which requires peaceful cooperation. The rise of total war in the modern age is due to the rise of "statolatry" and interventionism.

Chapter XXXIV: The Economics of War 329

Technical Notes

(1)   Mises's discussion (pp. 818–19) of the "war to abolish war forever"—in reference to Europeans at the time of Napoleon!—shows that more modern slogans are nothing new.

(2)   It is unclear whether Mises is endorsing a U.S. program to produce synthetic rubber (p. 826). One should keep in mind, however, that private firms may quite rationally stockpile necessary supplies, and even develop alternative production techniques, due to the possibility of supply disruptions. Given that the government monopolizes military affairs, then, it would not be a contradiction for Mises to endorse such a program. His main point is that the German militarists were wrong for classifying the costs of substitutes as a purely bourgeois fiction.

Study Questions

1. TOTAL WAR

- What can best safeguard durable peace, according to the old British liberals and their continental friends?

Comment: "But this is merely circular reasoning. We call aggressive nationalism that ideology which makes for modern total war. Aggressive nationalism is the necessary derivative of the policies of interventionism and national planning."

- What has transformed the limited war between royal armies into total war, according to Mises?

- What is the essential condition for peaceful coexistence?

2. WAR AND THE MARKET ECONOMY

Comment: "It surrendered to the claim of the unions that the workers' real take-home wages should be kept at a height which would enable them to preserve in the war their prewar standard of living."

- Why did the shortcomings of the methods adopted for financing war expenditures make government control necessary?

- The transition from peace to war changes the structure of the market and makes readjustment

Chapter XXXIV: The Economics of War   *331*

indispensable. How does the readjustment of the market constitute a source of profit?

Comment: "What the incompatibility of war and capitalism really means is that war and high civilization are incompatible."

3. WAR AND AUTARKY

- What is meant by the doctrine of "Ersatz"? What are two theorems of this doctrine? Why are both theorems fallacious?

4. THE FUTILITY OF WAR

Comment: "Economic nationalism, the necessary complement of domestic interventionism, hurts the interests of foreign peoples and thus creates international conflict."

- Why isn't the construction of new and dreadful weapons the root of evil? What is the real source of war?

Comment: "To defeat the aggressors is not enough to make peace durable. The main thing is to discard the ideology that generates war."

CHAPTER XXXV

THE WELFARE PRINCIPLE VERSUS THE MARKET PRINCIPLE

Chapter Summary

1. THE CASE AGAINST THE MARKET ECONOMY

Even critics of the market economy must admit that it works satisfactorily day in and day out, and indeed increases standards of living for everyone over time. Now the fashionable critique of the market is that it aims for profit, in contrast to "welfare." Broadly defined, no one objects to the welfare of others, but the term becomes vacuous; both liberals and Nazis can claim their programs aim to achieve as much happiness as possible. In the end, the modern welfare economists' critique of the pure market economy centers on three of its alleged characteristics: poverty, inequality, and insecurity.

2. POVERTY

Many utopian writers envision a society where everyone owns a piece of soil large enough to provide for himself. The problem with such an arrangement is that it cannot last; population growth ensures that heirs receive ever smaller portions of land, or that society becomes divided into the landowners and a growing population of disinherited paupers. In the ages before

333

the rise of modern capitalism, it was precisely these "excess" workers whom the statesmen and philosophers meant by "the poor." There was truly no place for these people in the social structure of the day.

This all changed with the rise of laissez-faire capitalism and the industrialization it fostered. Now the destitute beggars could work in factories and support themselves. In modern times, the mass poverty that persists in certain countries is due, first, to their relatively low capital per capita, but ultimately to their failure to embrace capitalism. Even the laborers of the West live as aristocrats compared to the average person elsewhere in the world.

Even under capitalism, there are invalids who cannot sustain themselves. Ironically, the very success of capitalism has allowed people to survive (in need of care from others) who would have perished in earlier ages. The funds to provide for such people have historically come from governments, but also from private charities, often organized through religious organizations.

Charity is criticized for its inadequacy. Yet interventionism itself weakens private charitable efforts, through the creation of mass unemployment, destruction of savings through inflation, etc. Charity is also criticized for its demeaning effects on the recipients. Yet here the interventionist contradicts himself, for it is precisely the "businesslike," contractual dealings in the marketplace—devoid of the personal element—that he also loathes. The substitution of a legal "right" to sustenance removes the incentives for people to support themselves, and it is questionable whether dependence on the whims of bureaucrats is less degrading than dependence on the mercy of philanthropists.

3. INEQUALITY

Inequality in incomes and wealth is an inherent feature of the market economy; to insist on equality would destroy the

Chapter XXXV: The Welfare Principle Versus the Market Principle   335

market. In practice, those calling for equality merely want to seize the incomes of those earning more than the reformers; American workers do not intend to share their incomes with the 95 percent of the world who earn less than they do.

Historically, some writers attacked the privileges of the traditional caste system because of a belief in natural rights and the metaphysical equality of all men. The utilitarians and economists also endorsed the equality of men before the law, but this was a pragmatic goal, necessary to allow the most able producers to best satisfy the wants of consumers. The economists understood that some men were far more capable than others, and this was precisely why the meritocracy of capitalism was necessary: to allow them to exercise their superior talents.

The explanation for the stagnation of the oriental and Muslim countries, despite their head start over Western Europe, is that the autocratic rulers of the former regions did not allow their subjects to amass large fortunes. They implemented the ideal of material equality, while the capitalist countries tolerated vast inequality in personal income and wealth.

The only path to rising standards of living is continual increases in the amount of capital per capita. Even though individuals may save only to "selfishly" provide for their future consumption (or for their heirs), even so they provide a service to all by increasing the supply of capital goods and hence raising the productivity of labor. Interventionism erodes or even completely reverses this tendency. Governments tax private wealth and substitute "social-security" provisions instead. Yet these do not consist in genuine savings, but merely in IOUs drawn on future taxpayers. The private citizen's abstinence from consumption does not expand the supply of capital goods, because it is (partially) siphoned away into government expenditures on consumption goods.

336   *Study Guide to Human Action*

The complete absence of considerations of the supply of capital goods in their policy recommendations should disqualify the welfare economists from even being classified as economists at all.

4. INSECURITY

In one sense, it is true that capitalism gives rise to the "insecurity" of income and wealth that its critics abhor. Yet this insecurity is not the fault of the capitalists, but rather of the consumers. The consumers each day seek those products and services that best satisfy their wants at the lowest prices. This is why successful producers are always at risk of failure: because each day they must outcompete their rivals anew.

The idyllic descriptions of earlier ages were false in this respect; no modern worker would trade places with a medieval farmer. And the insecurity of the Great Depression was caused by interventionism, not laissez-faire.

5. SOCIAL JUSTICE

In one respect the modern welfare theorists are superior to older schools of reformers. The modern propagandists at least acknowledge that the only metric for a social system is their ability to allow men to achieve their ends.

Even so, once they begin their critique of the market economy, the modern welfare theorists smuggle in their prejudices and ultimately fall back on the vehicle of a superhuman dictator who can always achieve superior outcomes versus the market populated by mere mortals.

The market economy has allowed an unprecedented growth in population, coinciding with an unprecedented growth in living standards. The welfare schools' criticisms of modern society prove only that scarcity exists and that people would benefit

Chapter XXXV: The Welfare Principle Versus the Market Principle   *337*

from more consumption. These observations do not impugn capitalism, the system that can best conquer these "problems."

Why It Matters

In this important chapter, Mises relies on the economic theory developed earlier in the book, in order to defend capitalism from the three recurring claims that provide the foundation for virtually all of its critiques: the existence of poverty, inequality, and economic insecurity under capitalism.

Technical Notes

(1) Mises writes,

> If the Englishmen of the eighteenth century had been preoccupied with the chimera of income equality, laissez-faire philosophy would not have appealed to them, just as it does not appeal today to the Chinese or the Mohammedans. In this sense the historian must acknowledge that the ideological heritage of feudalism and the manorial system contributed to the rise of our modern civilization, however different it is. (p. 838)

In the surrounding pages, Mises explains that the Chinese had enshrined the ideal of material equality far more than England. (Despite an autocrat, all of the subjects were equal under him.) Ironically, Mises is arguing that the gross inequality of feudalism allowed the Western peoples to tolerate its existence under modern capitalism, and thus benefit from this new social arrangement.

(2) In an interesting footnote (p. 842, n. 5) Mises writes, "To establish this fact"—namely, that the maintenance of the capital structure requires abstinence from current consumption—

> is, to be sure, not an endorsement of the theories which tried to describe interest as

Chapter XXXV: The Welfare Principle Versus the Market Principle   *339*

the "reward" of abstinence. There is in the world of reality no mythical agency that rewards or punishes.

Here Mises is criticizing the so-called abstinence theory of interest, which explained the phenomenon of interest as a reward to the painful postponement of consumption on the part of savers. Böhm-Bawerk too gave a lengthy critique of this theory. Of course, both Böhm-Bawerk and Mises thought the true explanation of interest was the higher subjective valuation of present versus future goods.

(3)   Mises cleverly explodes the glib defense of government debt that claims, "We owe it to ourselves." As Mises points out (pp. 843–44), the taxpayers who must fund government obligations are not the same ones who enjoy its spending.

Study Questions

1. THE CASE AGAINST THE MARKET ECONOMY

Comment: "A principle that is broad enough to cover all doctrines, however conflicting with one another, is of no use at all."

2. WAR AND THE MARKET ECONOMY

- What system is Mises describing with this quote: "The inherent weakness of such a society is that the increase in population must result in progressive poverty."

- What distinguishes the West from Asia with regard to the capital invested per person? What are the consequences of the lack of capital invested?

- Why is it false to blame the European powers for the poverty of the masses in the colonial countries?

Comment: "Within the frame of capitalism the notion of poverty refers only to those people who are unable to take care of themselves."

- Under capitalism, who cares for those who are handicapped by bodily incapacity?

- What are the two main alleged defects of charity?

- Which incentives are eliminated by the social-security system?

3. INEQUALITY

- Why would the elimination of the inequality of incomes and wealth destroy the market economy?

Comment: "The most despotic system of government that history has ever known, Bolshevism, parades as the very incarnation of the principle of equality and liberty of all men."

- Why has the principle of equality under the law been chosen by the liberals?

- What is wrong with the argument that the public debt is no burden because "we owe it ourselves"?

Comment: "Spending and unbalanced budgets are merely synonyms for capital consumption."

4. INSECURITY

Comment: "A characteristic feature of the unhampered market is that it is no respecter of vested interests."

- What is the explanation of the events of 1929, according to Mises? Why is this date important with regard to the question of security?

5. SOCIAL JUSTICE

Comment: "Their last word is always state, government, society, or other cleverly designed synonyms for the superhuman dictator."

- Why doesn't the market economy need apologists and propagandists?

CHAPTER XXXVI

THE CRISIS OF INTERVENTIONISM

Chapter Summary

1. THE HARVEST OF INTERVENTIONISM

All of the negative consequences of interventionism, predicted by the economists, have come to fruition. Yet it is not the world wars, depressions, famines, and civil wars that have led to the crisis of interventionism. On the contrary, these calamities have been blamed on capitalism. Even so, interventionism is reaching its end, because it has exhausted all its potentialities.

2. THE EXHAUSTION OF THE RESERVE FUND

The essence of interventionism is to lavish generous benefits and spending on the working classes, while requiring employers or "the rich" to pay for these items. Besides their other deleterious consequences, by the mid-20th century, these schemes had reached their logical fulfillment in Europe and had almost reached such a point in the United States. The reserve fund—the wealth of the rich, and the incomes of the entrepreneurs or "management"—had been drained, such that any new government spending or imposition on business would clearly be borne by the general public.

343

3. THE END OF INTERVENTIONISM

There are three reasons interventionism must come to an end. First, restrictive measures by their very nature cannot constitute a system of production. Second, all varieties of intervention in the market fail to achieve the very ends sought by their authors. These failures in turn spur only further intervention. Third, interventionism aims at seizing the "surplus" from one group and giving it to another; once the surplus is gone, interventionism must end.

By the mid-20th century, most of the European countries had adopted socialism of the German pattern, i.e., where private citizens retained nominal ownership of the means of production, but the government engaged in central planning. Even though these countries suffered because of these policies, they could at least rely on the market prices generated in the remaining capitalist countries.

There is no inevitable force propelling men to choose the social system that leads to progress; relapse is always possible. What can be said is that people must choose between socialism and the market economy; no "middle-of-the-road" position is stable. If people around the world adopt socialism such that economic calculation becomes impossible, then the result would be complete chaos and the disintegration of social cooperation.

Why It Matters

In this sobering chapter, Mises argues that interventionism is not a viable system because the "surplus" wealth of the rich capitalists will eventually be siphoned away. In the long run, people must choose between a market economy or outright socialism.

Chapter XXXVI: The Crisis of Interventionism 345

Technical Notes

(1) With the benefit of hindsight, it is an interesting exercise to evaluate Mises's claims. In the case of the United States, one might argue that the trend towards socialism advanced into the 1970s and then reversed its course afterwards, at least in certain respects. Even so, by many measures, the United States government in the 21st century is far more powerful than ever before.

(2) It may surprise the reader to see that Mises describes Great Britain as a socialist nation, and moreover that Winston Churchill presided over this transition (p. 855).

Study Questions

1. THE HARVEST OF INTERVENTIONISM

Comment: "Interventionism has exhausted all its potentialities and must disappear."

2. THE EXHAUSTION OF THE RESERVE FUND

- What is the essence of interventionist policy?

Comment: "From day to day it becomes more obvious that large-scale additions to the amount of public expenditures cannot be financed by 'soaking the rich,' but that the burden must be carried by the masses."

3. THE END OF INTERVENTIONISM

- What are the three reasons that will lead interventionism to an end?

- What three statements can be made about the struggle between the principles of private ownership and public ownership?

CHAPTER XXXVII

THE NONDESCRIPT CHARACTER OF ECONOMICS

Chapter Summary

1. THE SINGULARITY OF ECONOMICS

Economics is different from other branches of both pure knowledge and its practical utilization, because its theorems cannot be proven or falsified by experience. Naturally, action informed by faulty economic theories will be unsuccessful, but even here the failure will be shrouded in complex historical events. The economist can never definitely refute the economic cranks and charlatans in the same way that a doctor can refute a medicine man or snake-oil salesman. For example, a Keynesian can view the historical chronology of the Great Depression, and come away feeling that his theories are vindicated by "the facts." Such self-delusion is much harder to maintain in the experimental natural sciences.

2. ECONOMICS AND PUBLIC OPINION

Economics differs from other branches of knowledge in another respect: in order for the insights of the economic theorists to improve civilization, it is first necessary for the theorists (or popularizers) to convince the majority of the public. A

347

348   *Study Guide to Human Action*

pioneer in another field can proceed while the majority laughs at him; in the end, his successful results will speak for themselves. But sound economic policies cannot be implemented by a few outstanding thinkers; all governments ultimately rely on public opinion. The brilliance of a few economic theorists is irrelevant if the public clings to fallacious doctrines.

3. THE ILLUSION OF THE OLD LIBERALS

The liberal philosophers of the Enlightenment made one fatal mistake: they assumed that the great majority would support capitalism because of its undeniable benefits and their (assumed) ability to reason correctly. The old liberals failed to anticipate the success of anticapitalist propaganda, specifically the ability of Marxists to convince the masses of even the Western countries of their progressive immiseration—contrary to obvious facts.

Why It Matters

In this short chapter, Mises provides a springboard for those wishing to advance the ideas of liberty laid out earlier in the book. The twin difficulties facing such reformers are that (1) historical experience cannot "refute" bad economic doctrines, and (2) the majority must be convinced before sound economic policies can be implemented.

Technical Notes

(1) On page 858, Mises makes it clear that correct praxeological theorems, though established through a priori reasoning, are nonetheless of practical value to acting man. This point may seem obvious, but many critics of praxeology falsely interpret Mises to be claiming that praxeology is of no use in "the real world."

(2) Mises writes,

> The masses . . . do not conceive any ideas, sound or unsound. They only choose between the ideologies developed by the intellectual leaders of mankind. But their choice is final and determines the course of events. (p. 860)

This is a nuanced position in the strategic debate for advancing liberty. Some argue that modern supporters of the free market should aim to convert the intelligentsia, while others claim that it is more important to target the common person. Mises here does not settle the dispute but clarifies that economic policies are ultimately dependent on the views of the general public—views however that are adopted based on those promulgated by the elites.

Study Questions

1. THE SINGULARITY OF ECONOMICS

- Why aren't economic theorems open to falsification or verification by experience?

2. ECONOMICS AND PUBLIC OPINION

Comment: "The supremacy of public opinion determines not only the singular role that economics occupies in the complex of thought and knowledge. It determines the whole process of human history."

- On which factors does the flowering of human society depend?

3. THE ILLUSION OF THE OLD LIBERALS

- Which fact had been neglected by the old liberals with regard to public opinion? What were its consequences?

CHAPTER XXXVIII

THE PLACE OF ECONOMICS IN LEARNING

Chapter Summary

1. THE STUDY OF ECONOMICS

It is a mistake to believe that establishing an institute for business-cycle research can shed light on cures for the business cycle in the way that expensive funding for a cancer institute might discover a cure for the disease. Economists do not disagree on the relevant historical facts; where they disagree is on the a priori theories used to interpret these facts of economic history.

The Historical School and the Institutionalists wanted to displace economic theory and put "empirical" studies in its place, precisely because they could not refute the laissez-faire conclusions of the economic theorists.

What is needed for sound economic theory is not lavish spending by large organizations, but clear thinking.

2. ECONOMICS AS A PROFESSION

The early economists did not view economics as a profession; they wrote books and gave lectures solely to guide their fellow citizens in supporting sound economic policies. In modern

351

times, the rise of economics as a profession is an offshoot of interventionism. Governments, labor unions, big business, and other organizations rely on economists to guide their interventionist policies. Although many of these professional economists are eminent individuals, their talents are narrowly directed to advancing the interests of the small group that they advise.

3. Forecasting as a Profession

The recurrent boom-bust cycles caused by credit expansion naturally led businesses to employ economists for assistance in predicted the turning point. However, economists know only that the bust must follow the malinvestments engendered by the boom; they cannot predict the precise timing of events. Furthermore, the successful entrepreneur needs not merely accurate forecasts but forecasts better than those of his rivals. If everyone knew the date of the business downturn, no one could profit from such knowledge.

4. Economics and the Universities

University professors feel pressured not only to teach but also to engage in original research. In economics, however, at any time, there are only a score of thinkers who can actually advance economic theory. Consequently, the thousands of academics engage in compartmentalized analyses of "labor economics," "international economics," and so forth, even though in reality economics is a unified whole; there cannot be specialists the way surgeons specialize in the heart or brain.

Ironically, the most consistent students see through the fallacies of interventionism preached by their professors. They take their teachings to their logical conclusion and support socialism.

Chapter XXXVIII: The Place of Economics in Learning

5. GENERAL EDUCATION AND ECONOMICS

Everyone recognizes the impossibility of true neutrality in the schools in the area of religion; the liberals adopted the separation of church and state for precisely this reason. Yet the conflict exists also in history and economics. Most students are too immature to be presented with various interpretations among which they must choose, and, in any case, not enough teachers could be found to present the competing views in a neutral fashion. The only reason the political parties do not fight even more aggressively over control of the public schools is that citizens derive their views even more from other sources, such as the media.

6. ECONOMICS AND THE CITIZEN

In the 16th and 17th centuries, the main political controversies centered on religion. In the 18th and 19th centuries, the issue was representative government versus royal absolutism. In the 20th (and it appears the 21st) century, virtually all political controversies revolve around economics, namely, the conflict between socialism and the market economy. Consequently, the modern citizen has a duty to familiarize him or herself with basic economic theory.

7. ECONOMICS AND FREEDOM

Modern governments are adamant in suppressing the freedom of economic thought. Politicians and pundits behave as if the preceding centuries of economic analysis did not exist. In the face of such odds, all reasonable people can do is persevere and try to show the truth to enough of their fellows.

354   *Study Guide to Human Action*

Why It Matters

In this chapter, Mises discusses the historical evolution of economics from a vocation into a profession. His description of economic education at both the elementary and university level remains accurate to this day. This chapter, along with the previous one, assists the proponent of Misesian theory in understanding the difficulties to be faced in spreading correct ideas.

Chapter XXXVIII: The Place of Economics in Learning 355

Technical Notes

(1)   Mises writes,

> The natural sciences are ultimately based
> on the facts as established by laboratory
> experiment. Physical and biological theo-
> ries are confronted with these facts, and are
> rejected when in conflict with them.
> (p. 863)

Although useful as a foil with which to contrast
the nature of economics, this passage may mislead some readers. Even the "facts" of laboratory
experiments are theory laden; scientists cannot
help but rely on antecedent theories when interpreting their observations.

(2)   Mises writes,

> In countries which are not harassed by
> struggles between various linguistic groups
> public education can work very well . . .
> (p. 872)

In other works, Mises elaborates on his view that
linguistic barriers determine who wields the
political power in a country. In polyglot regions,
therefore, there are fierce battles over the
schools.

Study Questions

1. THE STUDY OF ECONOMICS

- What is the radical epistemological difference between the natural sciences and the sciences of human action?

- Which insights of economic history can be helpful for economics as such?

Comment: "Economics, like logic and mathematics, is a display of abstract reasoning."

2. ECONOMICS AS A PROFESSION

- What is the connection between the professional economist and interventionism?

- How does interventionism imply that a political career is only open to people who identify themselves with the interests of a pressure group?

3. FORECASTING AS A PROFESSION

- What would it imply if it were possible to calculate the future state of the market?

- What distinguishes businesspeople from statisticians with regard to the uncertainty of the future?

4. Economics and the Universities

- What observations does Mises make regarding tax-supported universities and their recruitment policy?

- What are the objectives of universities?

- What does scholastic tradition require?

- Why is it useless to divide economics into different branches? Why is there only one coherent body of economics?

Comment: "However, what has made many of the present-day universities by and large nurseries of socialism is not so much the conditions prevailing in the departments of economics as the teachings handed down in other departments."

5. General Education and Economics

Comment: "[In the domestic aspects of history, the] teacher's or the textbook author's own social philosophy colors the narrative."

- Why does general education only play a minor role in the formation of the political, social and economic ideas of the rising generation?

6. Economics and the Citizen

- What is the primary civic duty in our age, according to Mises?

7. ECONOMICS AND FREEDOM

Comment: "Prices, wage rates, interest rates, and profits are dealt with as if their determination were not subject to any law."

CHAPTER XXXIX

ECONOMICS AND THE ESSENTIAL PROBLEMS OF HUMAN EXISTENCE

Chapter Summary

1. SCIENCE AND LIFE

According to some critics, science is sterile because it is value free. Yet science provides humans with the information they need in order to properly form their valuations, and to choose the proper means to achieve their desired ends. From a philosophical view, it is true that all action is "vain," because people are never fully satisfied. Even so, they still act in order to achieve a more satisfactory state of affairs.

2. ECONOMICS AND JUDGMENTS OF VALUE

In conjunction with the above criticism—that economics is value free when it ought to show people how to live—there is the opposite one, that economists smuggle value judgments into their analyses. Economists themselves are partly responsible for this confusion. If an economist says that a price control is a "bad" policy, he is on scientific grounds only if he really means that this policy will not achieve its stated objectives. Similarly, the economist can recommend the market economy only if it is assumed that the objective is widespread prosperity and peace.

359

Another common objection is that economists assume people are only concerned with material well-being, when in reality people care about "irrational" objectives as well. This objection is baseless, because economics deals with action as such; there is no assumption that the action is directed toward material ends.

3. Economic Cognition and Human Action

Human freedom to act and choose is restricted in three ways. First, there are the physical laws of nature. Second, there are the individual's innate constitutional characteristics and environment. Third, there is the regularity of phenomena due to the connection between means and ends.

It is this third restriction on unbounded human choice that is the subject of praxeology. If people ignore its teachings, they will not annul economics, but they will stamp out society and the human race.

Why It Matters

In this final chapter, Mises reminds the reader of the nature of economics and its connection to ultimate judgments of value. He ends by warning that ignorance of the teachings of economics may literally result in the demise of humanity itself.

Technical Notes

(1) Mises writes,

> If an economist calls minimum wage rates a bad policy, what he means is that its effects are contrary to the purpose of those who recommend their application. (p. 879)

Mises's follower Murray Rothbard would amend this analysis. In fact, many of the politicians and bureaucrats implementing interventionist policies achieve their desired goals—namely, winning elections or receiving larger budgets.

(2) Another distinction between Mises and Rothbard is that Mises believed value judgments were ultimately beyond rational analysis (e.g., pp. 879–81). Rothbard rejected the so-called *is-ought* distinction, and thought that reason could shed light on the proper goals of humans. Even so, Rothbard agreed that *praxeology* was properly a value-free science.

Study Questions

1. SCIENCE AND LIFE

- What is meant by *Wertfreiheit*? How is it considered in modern science?

Comment: "Science does not value, but it provides acting man with all the information he may need with regard to his valuations."

Comment: "The subject matter of praxeology is merely the essential manifestation of *human* life, viz., action."

2. ECONOMICS AND JUDGMENTS OF VALUE

- In what sense can an economist call a policy good or bad?

- How does the economist answer the objection that people do not always strive for material well-being?

- In what way is economics apolitical or nonpolitical?

3. ECONOMIC COGNITION AND HUMAN ACTION

- How is man's freedom to choose and to act restricted?

Comment: "But if they fail to take the best advantage of it and disregard its teachings and warnings, they will not annul economics;

Chapter XXXIX: Economics & the Essential Problems of Human Existence 363

they will stamp out society and the human race."

Comment: "Prices, wage rates, interest rates, and profits are dealt with as if their determination were not subject to any law."

INDEX

Action
    definition of, 1
    individual and changing features
      of, 13
    prerequisites of, 1–2
    uncertainty and, 45
Anarchismm, 68
Appraisement, 134
A priori
    character of praxeology , 11
    definition of, 15
    relation to reality, 12
Association
    law of, 65–66

Banking
    free, 158–59, 163–64
Barter agreements
    Nazi, 306–07
Barter economy, 86
Bureaucracy, 120
Business cycle. *See* Trade cycle

Calculation
    and the market, 88
    as basis of civilization, 80, 82
    impossibility under socialism, 263
    problem of, 87–88
    relation to capital, 101
    scope of, 93–94

Capital
    accumulation , 229
    consumption, 181–82
    link to calculation, 101, 116
Capital goods
    convertibility, 180
    definition of, 116
    in production structure, 177–78
Capitalism
    as Marxist smear term, 101
    basis of civilization, 116
    relation to big business, 116–17
Cash balance, 153
Catallactics. *See* Economics
Competition
    social versus natural, 117–18
Conception, 13–14
Consumer sovereignty, 117, 136–37,
    227
Copyright, 137, 247
Corporativism, 320–21
Cost
    accounting , 135
    definition of, 30
    external, 247, 248
Credit
    contraction, 211–12
    expansion, 205, 209–12, 304–05

Darwinism, 67
Deflation, 156, 211–12

365

Democracy
    case for, 64
    "industrial," 319–20
Devaluation, 303–04
Dualism
    methodological, 3

Economics
    as profession, 351–52
    citizen and, 353
    Crusoe, 87
    education and, 353
    freedom and, 353
    judgments of value and, 359–60
    mathematical, 135, 265
    public opinion and, 347–48
    scope of, 105
    singularity of, 347
    study of, 351
    universities and, 352
Economy
    Market. *See* market economy
    progressing, 108, 119–20
    retrogressing, 108
    stationary, 108
Entrepreneurship, 119–20, 133–34
Equilibration, 134
Evenly rotating economy, 108, 196,
    241
Exchange
    action as form of, 30
    autistic, 79, 107
    interpersonal, 79
    media of, 151
Externalities
    negative, 247, 248
    positive, 247, 248

Fiduciary media, 158
Foreign exchange control, 305–06
Freedom, political versus economic,
    118

Game theory, 47, 49
Genius
    creative, 56, 59
God
    relation to liberalism, 64
    relation to praxeology, 4–5
    relation to society, 63
Gold standard, 161–62, 301
Goods
    consumers', 29
    first- and higher-orders of, 29–30
    free, 29
    non-material, 30
    producers', 29
Gresham's law, 292, 302

Harmony of interests, 252
History
    as science of human action, 11
    scope and method of, 13
Homo oeconomicus, 248
Human action. *See* Action

Ideal types, 14
Ideology, 73–75
Idle capacity, 139, 214
Imaginary construction, 86, 105–06
Income
    distribution, 139
    inequality, 334–35
Individualism
    methodological, 12
Industrial Revolution, 229
Inflation, 156

Instincts
    of aggression and destruction,
      66–67
    serviceableness of, 4
    versus action, 2
Interest
    components of gross rate of,
      206–07
    originary, 193–95
    neutral rate of, 205
    relation to time preference, 193
Interventionism, 271–72, 343–44
Investment, 183–84

Labor
    definition of, 55
    disutility of, 55
    division of, 63, 65, 66
    extroversive, 223–24
    immediately gratifying, 56
    introversive, 223–24
    mediately gratifying, 56
    slave, 231
    unionism, 294–95
Laissez faire, 273
Land
    as standing room, 240–41
    definition o, f240
    pricing of, 241
    reform, 313–14
    submarginal, 240
Legal tender legislation, 302
Liberalism
    and case for democracy, 64
    and peace, 326
    relation to gold standard, 161,
      301
    relation to praxeology, 64

Loss
    definition of, 31
    source of, 251

Malinvestment, 210
Marginal utility
    law of decreasing, 53–54
Market economy
    as affected by trade cycle, 213–14
    autonomy of, 291–92
    case against, 333
    characteristics of, 115
    pure, 106–07
    war and, 326–27
Means-ends framework, 29
Money
    as solution to calculation prob-
      lem, 87
    definition of, 151
    demand for and supply of, 152–53
    fiat, 157
    "hard," 302
    purchasing power of, 152
Monopoly
    of demand, 137
    price, 136

Patent, 137, 247
Polylogism, 23–25
Poverty, 333–34
Praxeology
    aprioristic character of, 11
    definition of, 1
    prediction with, 47–48
    versus history, 11
Price
    and production, 139
    controls, 292–93
    definition of, 30

determination, 133–34
discrimination, 138
nonmarket, 139
stabilization of, 94–95
Probability
case, 45–47
class, 45–47
meaning of, 45–46
Production
factors of, 29
mass, 230
period of, 175, 178–79
relation to action, 56–57
restriction of, 283–85
Productivity
marginal, 225
Profit
entrepreneurial , 119–20
maximization, 106–07
source of, 251
Property
private, 252–53

Rationality
relation to action, 3
Reason
as feature of man, 73
case for, 25
revolt against, 23
Regression theorem, 162, 163
Rent, theory of, 239
Returns
diminishing, 55
law of, 54
Ricardo effect, 296–97

Saving
and accumulation, 177, 183–84
forced, 208–09

Scale of value, 30, 53
Services
definition of, 30
Singularism
methodological, 13
Social justice, 336–37
Socialism
doctrine of, 258
guild, 320–21
impossibility of calculation under, 263
market, 265
origin of idea of, 257
patterns for realization of, 271–72
praxeological character of, 258
Society
definition of, 63
individual within, 66
State of rest
final , 107–08
plain, 107–08, 110
Stock market, 183, 186–87
Subjectivism, 3–4
Syndicalism, 319–20

Tariff, 284
Taxation
confiscatory, 314
neutral , 279
objectives of, 280
total, 279–80
Third system, 271
Time
factor in land utilization, 239–40
in praxeology, 37–39
maturing, 175
preference, 176
waiting, 178–79
working, 175
Trade cycle, 205

Index 369

Uncertainty
    acting and, 45
Understanding, 13–14
Unemployment
    catallactic, 226
    institutional, 294, 303
Utility
    definition of, 2

Wages
    definition of, 225
    determination of, 225
    gross and net rates of, 227
    iron law of, 227
    minimum rates of, 293–94
War
    market economy and, 326–27
    total, 325